IN THE SHADOW
OF
KINGS

By
DONNIE H. SUMNER

ISBN-9781469944029

Published By
LIFE LINE BOOKS
Hendersonville, TN 37075

Graphic Designs by
CRYSTAL DUNN
Crystal Inc. - Hixson, TN **37343**

Cover Photos by
RAY LEWIS
Lewis and Lewis, Hendersonville, TN **37075**

Editorial Assistants
**BILLY BARBER / ELIZABETH FORBIS
JOHN SCHAUBERGER / BILL SWOVELAND**

Dedication

*T*o ... **MY FAITHFUL WIFE**, Marty, the crowning jewel of my new life. Her prayers, love, support and encouragement have been the "wind beneath my wings" since 1983.

*T*o ... **MY SON AND DAUGHTER**, Jeff and Robin, who never gave up on "their Daddy" and continued to love me, when in truth, I wasn't worth their love.

*T*o ... **MY MOM AND DAD**, Rev. and Mrs. R. H. Sumner, whose exemplary lives and intercessory prayers kept the light of love shining bright enough to show me the way back home when my life had led me to the end of a hopeless road.

*T*o ... MY **BROTHER, PETE AND MY BROTHER-IN-LAW, ED FINCH,** who never passed up an opportunity to say, "Man! Hurry up and finish that book." ...

*T*o ... **EACH OF YOU**, along with my life long friends and my career fans:

*W*ith *ALL MY LOVE and SINCERE THANKS* ...
I DEDICATE THIS NARRATIVE!

A Note From Donnie

"Good evening ladies and gentlemen! Welcome to the Elvis Presley Show!!!"

With this line I opened over eight hundred exciting performances for my boss and friend, the late "Elvis."

Oh! By the way, My name's Donnie and music has been my life for over fifty years.

It's been quite an interesting road that has led me to this point.

By definition, a shadow is simply an effect resulting from a light source being directed toward an object and is only a resemblance of the form it replicates. In theological terms, the word "shadow" conveys the idea of "a protective covering."

I have been blessed to have had the opportunity to enjoy life in the shadow of several personalities of renown. Though not an exact duplicate of these individuals, I can assure you that "I AM" only because "THEY WERE."

In their respective genres of performance, I revere each of them as kings and highly cherish the memories we made together.

The only tools I have with which to bring those memories to life are a keypad and my computer.

As my fingers begin rendering the many scenes along my traveled past, they anxiously await the moment they will be able to proclaim, "I have truly been blessed!"

You're welcome to join me if you'd like. I'd be honored to have your company while I work.

4

Table Of Contents

IN THE SHADOW OF KINGS

CHAPTER ONE
An End At The Beginning

It's no wonder I was a mean kid! My Daddy was a Pentecostal preacher!

Daddy never would admit to my meanness. He chose to say I was mischievous. When questioned as to the source of my mischievous activities Dad would often reply, "I don't rightly know. He didn't git it from me, he's adopted, so, I guess it's from playin' with 'your' kids!" Any such statement would invariably be followed by a big smile.

Today I'm grateful for the heritage of being nurtured, trained and loved by two of the greatest examples of Christian living that one could ever have the privilege to know.

In October of 1943, at the ripe ole age of ten months, I was placed into the arms of Rev. and Mrs. Russell H. Sumner and for more days than I enjoy counting I have affectionately called them "Daddy and Momma."

Others might be hard pressed to label them as royalty. But as for me! By reason of the virtues they have exemplified and the love with which they have showered me, I stand flat footed and tell you, "Daddy and Momma have been the 'king and queen' of my life." They have been God's human hand reaching out to me sustaining and fortifying all the days of my living!

I was raised on Sunday School and Prayer Meeting. I wore clothes, ate food and lived in homes all financed by church money. Yes sir; I was "churchie" from top to bottom with the exception of the middle.

I have always worked at being different and unique, not only in my musical endeavors but in my life patterns as well. As a child I rebelled against the Christian regimen. I considered it to be a dull and over disciplined life style. I had bigger dreams and wider horizons than those I thought could be achieved by a devout Christian.

It took a lot of troubled days and many crooked paths but I have finally come to understand this truth: **"Train up a child in the way he should go: and when he is old, he will not depart from it."** *-Proverbs 22:16*

I think that I should probably take you all the way back to where the story began so that you can catch up to where I am today.

In a quiet little town in central Florida called Lakeland, on a chilly December 4th morning in the year 1942, I stepped onto the stage of life as **MARVIN HOWARD SUMNER**.

My biological parents, Frank and Irene Sumner now had three little ones they called "their kids."

In the thoughts of Frank and Irene, I choose to believe that things seemed to be at least a little brighter for them due to my uninvited arrival.

I can only imagine as to the opinions of the other immediate family members at the time.

Perhaps Frieda, the seven year old daughter of Irene by a previous marriage, was concerned because she was going to have the added responsibility of helping to keep quiet the noisy little "thing" she was looking at.

I'm sure that Franklin, the oldest child of Frank and Irene, known to our family as Pete, was not thinking about it at all because he refuses to worry and never loses sleep over anything.

And then there was Frances. Little Fran was the middle baby of Frank and Irene. Fran was only two years old when I was born and if she had an opinion, I'm sure she kept it to herself. She has always been the sweet and quiet child in our family.

By profession, Frank was a fruit picker and through the years, I have formed my own opinion about Frank from the stories told to me by those who knew him best. They all described him as a really likable sort of guy.

Those in our family who were closest to Frank tell me that he had three outstanding qualities. He loved his kids, sang well and worked hard.

They recall that five mornings a week the fruit company's flat bed truck would stop at the corner nearest our small apartment and Frank would jump aboard. They say that "ole Frank" would immediately sprawl out full length on his back and begin singing an old spiritual song that started off with, "Then cheer, my brother cheer, our trials will soon be o'er!"

In some of my quiet times I have thought, Just maybe, my love for gospel music was birthed on the back of an old worn out truck bed.

My brother Franklin, known to everyone by his nickname Pete has often related to me how Frank and Irene would supplement their meager income by playing their guitars and singing at various beer gardens in and around our little town of Lakeland.

I was fascinated to learn that Frank and Irene would often leave Pete and my sister Fran in the care of our older sister Frieda and head out for a musical and drinking appointment with Frank holding tightly to the handle of a large basket with "lil' ole me" tucked warmly inside. Pete has often told me that they would set my mobile nursery on the bar and then play and sing for as long as the tips kept coming in.

Frank and Irene must have been a really fun loving couple. I sure wish I had been afforded the luxury of knowing them but that opportunity was unexpectedly sealed in the tomb of time before I developed my ability to remember.

Frank had a weekend pastime. He never suspected that it would eventually affect his entire family. Frank loved to "drink."

On a warm July evening in 1943, Frank's best friend, John, stopped by our little lakeside apartment in South Lakeland to invite his buddy, Frank, to join him for a night on the town.

As always, Frank readily accepted the invitation and together they climbed into John's old pick-up truck and headed for their favorite hang out. It was just down the road in West Lakeland. Folks that frequented the establishment knew it as The Bluebird Inn.

Although a very short ride for them, it was destined to become a dividing mile in the lives of those Frank loved most.

As they entered the Bluebird, Frank and John were looking forward to a fun-filled evening and in just a short time, both were in full party mode.

With the passing of time, Frank and John became more and more intoxicated and they soon reached the point that the bartender refused to serve them any more drinks.

Having been refused any further service, Frank got into a rather brisk argument with the tavern owner. Their words quickly became a yelling and pushing altercation.

With a temper quotient much like mine used to be, Frank took a swing at the bar keeper and a full blown fistfight erupted.

During the commotion, John went behind the bar and helped himself to all of the cash in the bars cash register and then came dashing out. As he got to where Frank was, John grabbed Franks arm, pulling him away and together they ran through the front screen door and into the night.

Observing that the cash register was open and empty, the tavern owner rightly assumed that he had just been robbed by either or both, Frank and John.

The proprietor reached under the bar and solicited the help of his "associate bar keeper" … a pistol!

With pistol in hand, he ran out into the black of the evening in pursuit of Frank and John.

Earlier that evening it had started to rain and I have been told, that on that particular night, it was a frog strangler.

On a warm night in Florida, a heavy rain has a very unique characteristic. The darkness it creates makes it practically impossible to discern what is hidden in its shroud.

According to a news statement covering the event, "As the tavern owner peered into the darkness, the only thing discernible was a small patch of something white."

It was unfortunate that Frank had chosen to wear a white shirt that evening because when the gentleman raised his pistol and aimed, all that he saw was my Daddy's white shirt.

It only requires a slight squeeze to pull a guns trigger but that simple act of tightening the tension of one small finger totally and forever changed the lives of all those in the Sumner family.

Never expecting the impact, the bar keeper's bullet entered Frank's back and ripped out through a hole in his chest.

Just a few yards from the main highway, Frank, the father I never knew, died face down in a mid-summer, West Lakeland mud puddle.

The rainy night time darkness of July 2, 1943 blackened even deeper and for just about everyone in Lakeland it was simply the end of another day but for some of us, an uncharted path of life and living was just beginning.

Before the worlds were spoken into existence, God saw July 2, 1943 A.D.

When the time came, He permitted a young couple to enter this world, grow up, fall in love and become Russell and Nell Sumner.

He allowed all of this because He needed everything to already be in place when a little boy named Marvin was left fatherless.

He just wanted Marvin to have a wonderfully blessed life.

I'm Marvin and I have!

"Before I formed thee in the belly I knew thee ..." *-Jeremiah 1:5*

"Without a sunset there would never be a daybreak!"
-Donnie

11

CHAPTER TWO
Home Away From Home

"Why?"

Without a doubt, that question has to be the one most frequently asked during ones' lifetime.

I have often asked relatives, "Why did our mom put us kids up for adoption after our father was killed?" To date, no one has been able to satisfy my curiosity.

In fairness to a person I never knew, when I am asked the same question, I simply respond with, "I don't know."

Roughly, three months after Frank was killed, his brother, my Uncle Jimmy, received a phone call from our lady neighbor who gave him this message. "I was out on the porch and saw Frieda, Pete and Frances pushing Donnie in a baby carriage along the edge of our lake here. I got Donnie out and brought all four of them to my house. I can't get Irene to answer the door and I think someone in the family should come over and check on her."

Uncle Jimmy came over and found Irene intoxicated and passed out. He called the Bartow County Welfare Board who put him into contact with their Human Services Department. Together they set a time to meet Uncle Jimmy at our house.

That morning the authorities removed all four of us kids from our home and made us official wards of the court.

This action prompted Uncle Jimmy to make three phone calls. The first call was to Russell Sumner, Jimmy's first cousin. The next was to Robert Sumner, the father of both Jimmy and my dad Frank. The last call was made to another first cousin,

John Daniel Sumner, the brother of Russell Sumner.

Uncle Jimmy explained the situation to each of them. He asked if they would be willing to help out until better arrangements could be made and each of them said, yes without hesitation.

Unexpectedly, the four of us kids were about to find ourselves living in separate homes.

At the time, I'm sure Frieda didn't understand that she wasn't gonna see the rest of us for another fifty years.

Pete didn't realize that his farmer Grand daddy would soon become his very close dad.

Frances didn't know that her second cousin, John Daniel, would shortly be her daddy and that he would rise to become, J. D. Sumner of Gospel Music fame, as-well-as Elvis' closest friend.

I feel confident that Russell and Nell didn't foresee me calling them Daddy and Momma as they walked toward their car that afternoon with me in Nell's arms. I'm certain they had no inkling that, many years in the future, I would be standing on stage beside either Elvis Presley, the King of Rock music, J.D. Sumner, the King of Gospel music or Bill Gaither, the King of Inspirational Music performing in the huge Lakeland Civic Center that would eventually be erected directly across the street from the little apartment they were leaving.

It had been a long day and sunset was beginning to shadow Lakeland as Frieda, Pete, Frances and myself began our journeys along separate paths.

Like everyone, I have experienced periods of extreme complexity and uncertainty and have often faced situations that, in all probability, would have destroyed me. Through them all, the Lord of Glory has watched over me. He has shielded, protected and provided for me with His grace-filled sovereignty and I have been able to successfully overcome every traumatic moment.

"... The Lord is my rock, and my fortress, and my deliverer." -II Samuel 22.2

*In the end, the followers of "Jesus The Christ," **always win!***

"... If God be for us, who can be against us?" - Romans 8:31

"God is for me!" - Psalm 56:9

Can you determine who became his great uncle's grandson; Whose sister became his third cousin; Whose brother became his uncle; Whose second cousin became his daddy and who just might wind up being his own grand paw someday? It was **me!**

CHAPTER THREE

Same Face - New Name

"Short" is a relative word.

What was to be just a short time for us kids, turned into weeks and we were still being cared for by our respective custodial relatives.

For reasons that she alone will ever know, Irene chose to take Frieda, leave Lakeland and start her life over. For the next fifty years their lives would be a mystery to all of us.

When Irene left town, Grand daddy Bob, J.D. and Mary along with Russell and Nell each petitioned the courts for permanent custody of their respective wards.

Soon afterwards, Robert and Clifford Sumner were awarded their legal rights as parents to Pete. J. D. and Mary Sumner were named as the legal parents of Frances.

On May 17, 1944, the State of Florida declared lil' ole me, Marvin Howard Sumner, to be the legal son of Russell and Nell Sumner.

My new Mom and Dad didn't particularly like the name Marvin and I was their son now so why not choose a name for the kid that would better suit their liking?

Why it had to be, "**Donnie,**" I can't imagine but that's the name I've been stuck with ever since.

I truly wish that I had been blessed with the joy of growing up with my brother and sisters but it was not to be so.

Never-the-less, "God Is Good!"

I didn't know it at the time but waiting in the corridors of my future was another sweet, little sister named Sharon. She has been my buddy ever since she was adopted into our family when I was three years old and she was only five days old.

"But what ever happened to Frieda?" I'm glad you asked.

Through information that my uncle J.D. discovered, on my fiftieth birthday, December 4, 1992, in Pooler, Georgia, my brother Pete and I were able to reunite with our older sister, Frieda and for the first time since we could remember, us kids laughed, talked and had a family meal together.

I never had the opportunity to know Frank and Irene. My entire knowledge of their life is that which has been passed on to me and all that I have relayed to you.

I am assured of only two facts in their regard and both are by reason of visual proof.

My first observation was made with the help of my brother Pete when I was eleven years old. It was at my Grand daddy Bob's graveside ceremony. Pete led me over to a spot in the cemetery, pointed down and said, "That's where our Daddy's buried."

The other I witnessed the day Pete and I took Frieda back to her home in Pavo, Georgia in 1992. That afternoon Frieda led us down a dirt road to a tiny cemetery. She led us over to a marker and said, "Momma's buried right there." I think Pete's response mirrored my thoughts. "Well, Duck," he said, "We won't have to wonder anymore where Momma is!"

May I briefly state one additional fact for the record? I know that my name is **Donnie Howard Sumner**, I am the son of Rev. and Mrs. R. H. Sumner and I have a little sister named

Sharon and that, boys and girls, makes me one of the most fortunate and divinely blest men on planet earth.

The very "best things" I know for certain are these:

I know that I have been adopted by my Heavenly Father.

"... Ye have received the Spirit of adoption, whereby we cry, Abba Father." -Romans 8:15

I know I have all the legal rights of son-ship.

"And if children, then heirs; heirs of God and joint-heirs with Christ ..." -Romans 8:17

And I know that, someday, I will live in His Presence eternally, in a land where there will be no more graveyards.

"For God so loved the world, that He gave His only begotten Son, that whosoever believeth in Him should not perish, but have everlasting life." -John 3:16

My birth name Marvin was never legally changed to Donnie. The name, Donnie, only appears on public records and my career credits. The good news is, if I ever choose "not to be," I can "be not" because legally, "I don't exist."

CHAPTER FOUR

Church, Church and More Church

"Churchie" is a word not found in the dictionary but if Webster ever adds it, you'll see my picture beside the definition!

From the time I was adopted by my parents, until I left home in 1960, Church was the focal point of our existence. Everything revolved around our church life.

In 1947, Daddy resigned his position as superintendent of the largest fruit processing plant in Florida and entered the ministry. Having dropped out of school in the sixth grade, he felt the need to further his education, so, Daddy sold our house and bought a house trailer. With our new mansion being pulled behind a 1946 Pontiac, the Sumner family traveled to Cleveland, Tennessee where Daddy enrolled in Lee College, a Pentecostal Bible School.

It was less than a bed of roses in Cleveland. Daddy had a school load of twenty one semester hours and worked forty hours a week in a stove foundry. Momma spent all of her time doing washing and ironing for the college guys that could afford such a luxury. The only amenity that Sharon and I enjoyed was sharing a box of Cracker Jacks every Saturday when we went to the grocery store.

At that point in my life, I considered the words "poor and strict" to be synonymous with the title, "Christian." Sad to say but this perception continued throughout the major portion of my life and I wasted many years trying to outrun both The Church and the phrase, "Preacher's Kid."

Though I was only five, I was old enough to determine

one thing for certain, "I ain't 'never' gonna be a preacher."

Never say, never! God has an unusual sense of humor. He delights in leading folks into what He sees for them as good! The person I said I would never be, I now am!

I hated going to church for two major reasons: Momma dressed me like a nerd and Daddy preached too long!

At my Dads first revival during the summer of 1948, one of the other boys in the church made fun of my clothes and I got mad at him as well as Daddy and Momma. I was already sick of church and decided to run away from home. Right after breakfast the next morning I left the house that the church had provided for us and started my pilgrimage to, where God only knew! One thing was for certain, "I wasn't gonna go to church no more!"

As much as I hated getting back on a church pew, I sure am glad Daddy and Momma found me just before midnight that evening. Those woods were extremely dark and I was getting mighty scared. That could very well be the reason why I still sleep with a night light on.

As often as I was in church, I sometimes wonder how I had enough time to do anything else. The answer is simple! I didn't do much else! I ate, slept, attended school and went to church!

If the congregation met, we were with them! If the church sponsored an event, we participated! If the church approved it, we lived by it! If the church disapproved of it, we rejected it!

I often say, "I was as 'churchie as Noah was 'arkie'!" If anyone has ever been churchie I was but I sure didn't like it!

Considering now, the most important building blocks in my life, I am certain that the most important ones of these were having the heritage of a "church life," the love of a "close family," and the living example of a "Godly Dad and Mom."

"Train up a child in the way he should go: and when he is old, he will not depart from it." -Proverbs 22:6

During many sleepless nights since I began my new life, the memory of Momma's singing has come to mind and I was quieted by an unheard melody from the heart of my Heavenly Father. The soothing calm emitting from the invisible presence of His Holy Spirit has turned those, otherwise, fretful hours into evenings of an indescribable peace.

"I will both lay me down in peace, and sleep, for thou, Lord, only maketh me dwell in safety." -Psalm 4:8

"Thou wilt keep him in perfect peace whose mind is stayed on Thee ." -Isaiah 26:3

"It is good for a man that he bear the yoke in his youth."
-*Lamentations 3:27*

CHAPTER FIVE
A Dream Is Born

"**W**ow! That has to be the biggest car in the world." At least that's the way it looked to me as a six year old kid. To me it looked as long as a freight train.

Actually it was just a 1947 Cadillac limousine and it had just pulled to a stop in front of our home.

I use the term home loosely. In reality, it was a tiny, thirty-eight foot house trailer but as they say, "Home is where the heart is!"

My playground was a tar-covered alley that ran along one end of our trailer lot estate.

Directly across the big, one lane street, in front of our four trailer, subdivision lived an ugly creature known as the Mayfield Elementary School. Over the next couple of years I developed a strong dislike for that child eating monster!

That morning I was sitting on the couch at the front end of our trailer dreading another day in school. You might ask, "How do you remember your thoughts that day in light of your age at the time?" The answer is, I don't! On the other hand, I can't recall a single day of school that I ever looked forward to, so, I must assume that my outlook on that particular morning was the same as it was on every school morning that I do remember.

I sure got excited when that enormously long white car pulled to a stop in front of our trailer.

Very noticeably printed in big black Gothic letters on the

sides of both front doors and on the top of the trunk lid were words that read, "THE SUNSHINE BOYS - Wheeling, West Virginia."

I vaguely knew who the Sunshine Boys were but I knew that my Uncle Jake was one of them and I was up and off the couch and out the front door of the trailer in less than the proverbial minute because Uncle Jake was my hero!

Known now as "J. D. Sumner the world's lowest bass singer," my Uncle Jake had left his Southern Gospel Quartet group in Florida billed as The Sunny South Quartet and had joined The Sunshine Boys in 1946. Uncle Jake and the guys experienced a fast rise in popularity and had become a part of Wheeling, West Virginia's WWVA Jamboree a sister to Nashville, Tennessee's world renowned Grand Ole Opry.

I have yet to experience the joys of Heaven but at that age in my life I am certain that if I had been asked what Heaven was like, I would have quickly replied, "It must be like this!" Because nothing could possibly be any better than seeing Uncle Jake and listening to his stories.

Some of my most treasured memories of the grown ups in our family are those times when I recall sitting in their company, listening to tales remembered by them from a day gone by.

I have heard Uncle Jake talk about that day and I remember him describing the joyful experience of sharing his success with his brother as well as the pest I became in regard to his car.

I was accustomed to the cramped quarters of my Dad's '46 Pontiac coupe and I began begging Uncle Jake to show me his big long car. I suppose he became wearied by my nagging because he eventually opened the driver's door and said, "Jump in!"

What an experience! I had never seen anything like the inside of that limo.

There was a window inside the back of the front seat that could separate the front from the back and to my amazement it went up and down with the push of a button.

The rear window looked like it was a mile away and there were two little seats between the front seat and that far off back seat that could be folded up and down.

Little did I know that someday I would be sitting in a much newer limousine, perched on a similar fold up seat with Elvis Presley facing me from the rear seat as we were being chauffeured down Hollywood Boulevard.

I guess you might say, it was a long white limousine that caused me to make my first career choice. "Someday, I'm gonna grow up and when I do, I'm gonna be just like Uncle Jake."

I can honestly tell you, from that morning until September 5, 1965, not a single day passed without me finding myself, at some point, dreaming of the day I would walk onto a concert stage and sing in an all male, Southern Gospel Quartet, "just like" my Uncle Jake.

Dream on little dreamers! Dreams can and do come true!

When the Heavenly Father interacts with circumstances and makes a decision to rearrange the order of our life events according to His purpose and pleasure, the end result is always great!

**"Trust in the Lord with all thine heart;
and lean not unto thine own understanding.
In all thy ways acknowledge him,
and he shall direct thy paths." -Proverbs 3:4-6**

God sponsors "no flops!"

**"... we know that all things work together for good
to them that love God, to them who are the called
according to his purpose." -Romans 8:28**

"Dreams have no failures. Anything is possible in a dream."

-Donnie

CHAPTER SIX
Headin' South

When something has to give, it usually does.

In the Spring of 1951 my Dad had a physical breakdown!

During three and one half years of college work he was able to maintain a 3.0 grade average and that's remarkable in view of the fact that Daddy only had a sixth grade education. In addition to his studies, Dad was working a full time job and preaching on the weekends. Eventually, the stress overcame him and Dad dropped out of college.

The fall of that year found us en route to Bradley, Florida where my father had been appointed as the pastor of a small Pentecostal church. Once again, with our trailer behind us, the Sumners were relocating.

Topping the good list among the things I remember most about Bradley is the fact that, "there was no school house there!" The nearest institution for literary confinement was ten miles away.

Upon our arrival, Daddy pulled our trailer into a small cow pasture behind the little church and in the next few weeks he was able to refurnish our mobile estate.

We soon had a front porch added to our house. Daddy found some discarded railroad cross ties and he placed them side by side at the entrance to our trailer. The crowning touch came when one of the members gave Daddy an old piece of worn out linoleum to lay on top of the timbers.

We wouldn't have running water for over a year but as soon as Daddy got the porch finished, he personally drilled a water well and installed a pitcher pump on the pipe. Things were looking better now around the ole homestead.

We didn't really experience luxury until Daddy was able to build us a rest room. Suffice it to say, If our bathroom ever caught on fire there was no real danger. The fire could easily be extinguished before it got to our trailer!

Daddy's heartbeat was his family and his church! With the family, now relatively comfortable, he began improvements on the church.

As usual in those days, if work was to be done on the church the preacher had to do most of it and Daddy certainly did more than his share!

Dad's first order of business was to figure out a way to cool off the church and he was able to accomplish it by building his own air conditioning system. He cut a big square hole in the church ceiling and constructed a large cardboard air duct that reached from the hole to the end of the church attic. At that end of the duct work he installed an industrial fan. Daddy's plan was to open the windows and draw air into the building with his fan system. He didn't know how strong the air flow would be until the following Sunday when a sweet sister started jumpin' and shoutin' beneath the hole Dad had cut in the ceiling. I guess the joyful movements of the dear saint loosened her hat because the last time it was seen, it was flyin' thru a hole in the roof!

Daddy had his problems to deal with and so did I. Our denominational teachings were both numerous and very restrictive. In my young mind it seemed that the only word in the Bible was "don't!" and if I tried to live by all the "don'ts" I could only "do" one thing! Go to church and sit still!

When I was about eight, I sneaked off with a buddy of mine and went swimming in a public swimming pool. Momma found out about it and Daddy made me get up the next Sunday and apologize to the entire congregation. When I told them I was sorry, I knew I really wasn't. They didn't know it but I was already trying to figure out how I could get away with it the next time.

I got a serious spanking on one occasion when I got caught playing checkers with my next door buddy. I didn't understand why then and I still don't. All we had done was make a checker board out of cardboard and used Coke caps and Seven Up caps for checkers. Daddy thought I was bending over to accept my spanking but the truth is, I was bent over praying that he would never find out that I had played Old Maid cards with another buddy of mine.

Alone in the cow pasture playing cowboy was the way I spent most of my free time and I'll tell ya why, my Uncle Jake was a "real" cowboy!

J.D. and The Sunshine Boys had gone to Hollywood as singing cowboys on the Durango Kid movie series. Their first movie was Prairie Roundup. I had heard Uncle Jake talk about it but our church didn't believe in movie goin'. As much as I wanted to, I didn't reckon I'd ever get to see it.

One Saturday at the completion of my piano lesson in Lakeland, my cousin picked me up and informed me that Prairie Roundup was playing at the Polk Theater there in Lakeland. I really had a tough decision to make when he asked me to go with him to see it but after about two seconds of serious contemplation I replied, "O.K." and off to the movie we went. The best news is: Daddy never found out! That is, 'til now!

Bradley was quite a town. Since the time I left there, they have experienced a population explosion and now thrive as a metroplex maintaining over three hundred residents.

It took a long time for me to determine the fact but I have discovered far more "do's" in the Word of God than I have "don'ts!"

In trying to accomplish all of those "do's," I have realized that the "don'ts" become a non-issue.

"A certain lawyer stood up saying,
"Master, what shall I do to inherit eternal life?"
He said unto him,
"Thou shalt love the Lord thy God with all thy heart,
and with all thy soul, and with all thy strength,
and with all thy mind;
and thy neighbor as thyself.
This do, and thou shalt live." -Luke 10:25-28

"Home is like a pie. It 'is' what you make it!"
-Donnie

CHAPTER SEVEN
A Christmas Of Love

A little boy needs big heroes and I've been lucky! I've had two, my Dad and my Uncle Jake. Over the years I have become a composite of the two. They gave to me a love that was representative of the kind each member of our family had one for the other.

At no time in any given year was our family love more tangibly expressed than at Christmas time when we all gathered at grand mama's house for the big Sumner Christmas.

We usually had thirty to forty members of our family around the tree when we started opening gifts every Christmas Eve afternoon and I did say "afternoon!" You see, grand mamma wanted the gifts opened one at a time so she could squeal, "ooh" and yell, "save the bow" at each unwrapping. It always took four or five hours for her to have successfully bragged on all the presents.

The year after my Dad became pastor in Bradley, Christmas, 1952, came to our home and gift money was no where to be found but, as usual, we just had to go to grand mama's for the big Christmas.

With just enough cash for gas to put in our old Pontiac and with not enough money for a single gift to give, we set out for grand mama's.

We arrived safely and shortly thereafter it was time for us to open the presents.

At that time, Uncle Jake was still a member of the

Sunshine Boys Quartet. All of us in the family considered him to be a rich star. Though not self-appointed, by tradition he was our official Santa.

About an hour or so into the unwrapping frenzy, Uncle Jake noticed that no one had received a gift with the usual, "From Buddy, Nell, Donnie and Sharon."

Uncle Jake stood up, excused himself and called Daddy aside to talk to him. Only in my adult years did I become aware of the conversation they had that afternoon.

In their privacy, Uncle Jake said to Daddy, "Buddy, I know you're sort 'a short on cash and probably weren't able to buy gifts for everybody but by any chance were you able to get Donnie and Sharon anything from you and Nell?"

Just as he did when sharing this story with me, I'm sure Daddy got rather emotional and teary eyed when he replied to Uncle Jake with no expectations in mind, "Jake, I just didn't have the money and it's breaking my heart."

As they returned to the living room we received a saddening announcement from Santa. "Hey y'all! Cool it a bit. Me and Buddy's gotta take a break!"

It seemed like all afternoon but after a short wait Christmas resumed with great gusto. It was amazing that shortly thereafter, my sister smiled real big when Santa said, "To Sharon from Mom and Dad." Grand mamma let go with a big, "Ooh! What a pretty doll!"

Imagine my joy when I heard Santa say, "To Donnie from Mom and Dad." That was the first real bat, ball and glove I ever owned!

Those were the only two gifts Mom and Dad could afford that year.

"Thank you, Uncle Jake! You're gone but still loved!"

Thank God for the love of "Mom and Dad" and "Big Brothers!"

It sorta reminds me of my "Elder Brother, Jesus."

One Christmas long ago, God my "Heavenly Father" called Him aside and asked Him if He had anything to give me and He replied, "Only 'My Love' and 'My Life'."

Imagine, someone "loving me" enough "to die for me."

**"Greater love hath no man than this,
that a man lay down his life for his friends." -John 15:13**

I'm sure glad I'm in "God's family." and "my wish" is,
"That you are too!"

"God so loved the world, that he gave his only begotten Son."
-John 3:16a

CHAPTER EIGHT
Nothin' Happened

"**O**n this spot in 1886, NOTHING HAPPENED!"

I once saw that displayed on a sign that someone had posted in jest.

Their inscription was made to be funny but I write mine because it's true!

I can honestly say, that from August 1954, when we moved to Miami, Florida until 1960, when I left from home in Easton, Maryland, "nothing major happened!"

I got up every morning, went to school five days a week. I attended church twice on Sunday. I was back in church every Tuesday and Friday night as well as every service of every revival. I probably did more school homework on a church pew than I did in my own bedroom.

In school I looked funny, acted peculiar and was a basic nerd. Life continued on and so did my dislike for religion and discipline.

When I enrolled for school my first semester in Miami, they wanted me to take a class they called Cotillion. It was a program in which they taught ballroom dancing. I knew that Daddy wasn't gonna go for that and to tell them that my church didn't believe in dancing was too embarrassing for me.

So, I lied and told them, "I had polio when I was a baby and I can't do all that moving around!"

To this day, the only dancing I have ever done was as a

direct result of attitude adjustments being administered to the back side of my anatomy!

In the course of my life I have lived in twenty eight houses and the first nice home I can remember enjoying was in Crisfield, Maryland.

During the second year of his pastorate in Crisfield, Daddy was able to build a beautiful three bedroom parsonage and for the first time in my life I felt like I was as good as anybody but the joy only lasted for a few months.

In August of 1958, our denomination transferred my Dad to Easton, Maryland. As it turned out, that was to be my last moving experience with Daddy and Momma.

Easton was also the place where I finally defeated the child eating monster that first attacked me in Cleveland, Tennessee. After twelve hard years of fighting the creature, I finally watched him lay down in the dust and die. In 1960, I graduated from Easton High School, number "32" in a class of two hundred and forty students.

I have discovered that you can leave home but thoughts of home will never leave you.

Second only to my relationship with God, the greatest blessing in my life was having the opportunity to be the son of Rev. and Mrs. Russell H. Sumner. Since 1943, their prayers have been my covering, their example and teachings have been my benchmark and their love has been my rock.

The poor preacher eventually became an executive church leader and the mean kid finally became a man but to Russell and Nell, I will always be "our boy" and to me they will always be "Daddy and Momma!"

I love to laugh. I laugh at myself more than anything else. Laughing makes me feel better.

As a matter of fact, I've had several good laughs remembering the way things were when I was a kid.

It sure is great to enjoy laughing with a clear conscience.

"A merry heart doeth good like a medicine:
but a broken spirit drieth the bones." -Proverbs 17:22

"Laughter is like breathing.
You can't get by to long without it!"
-Donnie

CHAPTER NINE
Momma's Sugar

Times have changed, family members have dispersed and I have evolved into an old man with a family of my own but thru all the years of my growing up, one special thing has remained constant.

For as many years as I can recall, if we were lucky enough to be at our house for Christmas, as soon as the sun began to hide itself on Christmas eve, Mom, Dad, my sis and I would all find ourselves together around the Christmas tree that Mom had so humbly decorated. The tree was never fancy. It was usually decorated with trimmings made by my sister and I.

In anticipation of what was sure to come, Sharon, and I would settle down on the floor in front of Momma as Daddy picked up his Bible and began to read The Christmas Story from *Luke chapter 2.*

At the completion of Dad's reading, it was certain that Momma was going to begin singing Silent Night and that she expected everyone to join in.

Momma wasn't a great singer and would have never been invited to sing on stage with Elvis Presley but I can tell you, for a fact, that some of the sweetest music I have ever heard has come from the lips of the little lady I call Momma.

Though I have become a polished vocalist by some folks standard, I have yet to be able to render the melody of Silent Night as sweetly as Momma could.

The leaves have all fallen in my front yard, Christmas is coming on and as always, I'm kinda lookin' forward to the holidays.

I will probably get to hear Handel's Messiah again and I will for sure enjoy the laughter of my grand kids as we gather around our Christmas tree.

Daddy is enjoying Heaven now but hopefully, God's grace will allow me the joy of sharing another Christmas with my precious Mom.

At some point while in her presence, I am certain that the six-foot-three, two hundred and twenty five pound, sixty nine year old, "little boy" in me will have a strong urge to get up and once again go sit on momma's lap.

It sure would be nice to relax in her arms and listen to the sound of her voice as she sings Silent Night.

Thank God for Mommas.

With loving hands they bathe us, feed us, dress us, doctor us and discipline us. They rise early and go to bed late. They pray for us and wait patiently during the late hours of night for our safe return. Eventually they release our grown bodies into the hands of Divine Love.

As adults we make our own choices. Sometimes they are good and at other times, not so good.

Regardless of the paths we choose and the consequences that result, one thing remains constant: Momma will always be there with arms open and hands reaching out.

If Momma has ever kissed you one time, nothing else will ever replace it.

"You can't wipe off Momma's sugar!"

"Her children arise up, and call her blessed ..." *-Proverbs 31:28*

"Momma's love is like your shadow.
Every time you turn around it's there!
-Donnie

CHAPTER TEN
You Can't Fool A Mirror

"Idle hands are the devils work shop!"

Momma used that axiom frequently during my childhood days. It was her motivational tool for those times when I was engaged in "career assessment" otherwise known as "lazin' around!"

The truth of the matter is this! Idleness is the first step toward failure due to the fact that idleness begets nothing!

I have often been asked, "What was 'show business' like?" Well, the closest I can come to a description is this, it's like a yo-yo on a string. You just go back and forth, up and down with lots of idle time between the top and the bottom! The only rut you ever get in is not having a rut to get into and life without a rut has neither a route to follow nor any restraints to guide you as you travel the path to someplace.

I have often said, "You can't hitch hike with thumbs going in different directions! You will soon find out, you can't get there unless you know where there is." I know! I've been there!

Thankfully I can tell you that with Christ in my life I have come to know exactly Who I am, What I am and Where I am going!

Stars live in a world of illusion. You are a star only if the fans say you are! Your persona is the one created by the desires and opinions of your fan base.

Given enough time and success, a celebrities former identity becomes sequestered and they exist only as a clone of their fan base. At that point, their lifestyle has no real thread of reality connecting them to a normal life style.

For the most part, the world of showbiz is populated by citizens with imaginary profiles, relying on the support of outside influences to maintain their illusion during the idle times.

When a celebrity looks into his or her mirror they are forcibly reminded of their weaknesses and insecurities. No image in the mirror has the will or the strength to continually be what the face on a poster embodies. You can't fool a mirror!

Some find reinforcement in their power of influence over others. Some rely upon the temporary pleasures experienced in their pursuit for personal gratification. Others overcome their insecurities with personality altering substances such as alcohol and drugs.

In November of 1960, I found myself taking my first baby steps along a path that would become wider and rougher in the days that lay ahead. A road on which I would become more and more dependent upon my chosen support team, immorality and drugs!

In my wildest imagination, I could have never foreseen how far I would travel, how dark the nights would become nor how steep and jagged would be the chasm into which I would eventually fall.

Though I am not proud of all the details, if you wish to, you can remember with me and be an unseen observer as I try to retrace the route from my "old man" rocking chair.

I have discovered that if you know your business, remain honest and work hard; There is no career dream that cannot be realized and subsequently enjoy the fruit of.

Mistakes will be made but the object of the game is to "try again!"

Can you possibly imagine what kind of condition the world would have been in if the developer had quit when he created "6 UP." We would have never enjoyed the taste of a cold, "7 UP!"

"I count not myself to have succeeded:
but this one thing I do,
forgetting those things which are behind,
and reaching forth unto those things which are before,
I press toward the mark ..." -Philippians 3:13-14

"You can't 'fall up' the stairs,
you have to climb them one step at a time!"
                                                    -Donnie

40

CHAPTER ELEVEN
Off and Runnin'

"You're only in music because 'J.D.' is your uncle!"

A man once made that statement to me and through the years I'm certain there have been others who have wanted to voice the same opinion. To anyone who would have the nerve to entertain such a thought I say, "You're absolutely right!"

J.D. Sumner, the worlds lowest bass singer and my Uncle Jake was giving enough to share with me a place to begin my career. He was patient enough to help me build my dream. He cared enough to help me fulfill my dream and he loved me enough to enjoy the dream with me.

My childhood hero, J.D. Sumner, sure did cast a huge and wonderful shadow on my living.

Growing up, my dream was to be a singer like my Uncle Jake and the first time I touched the dream was the night I heard an emcee say, "Ladies and Gentlemen, would you welcome, The Songsmen!"

It was in October of 1960 and that was my first big time paying concert! Man, was I ever excited and my excitement was enhanced due to the fact that The Blackwood Brothers were on the same bill with us. The Blackwood Brothers were reputed to be the number one Gospel Quartet of the period and my Uncle Jake was their bass singer.

I look back on the event and realize that all four of us in the group were sure elated at being a quartet. I often tell folks that we even went to the restroom together so that everyone would know we were a quartet.

At some event, since then, I surely must have looked more handsome than I did that evening but at the moment, the memory of such an occasion eludes me You might have reason to disagree but it's "my story" and I'm gonna tell it the way I want to!

Often times during our first stand, I would look to the stage left wing and see my Uncle Jake standing there watching to see how I was gonna do. Every time I noticed his presence my chest would swell a couple more inches with overwhelming pleasure.

When my turn came for a solo, I remember singing the song, Then I Met The Master. The song begins as a story of one who's life had fallen apart and concludes with that same life being changed as a result of allowing The Christ to become his life's master. I didn't know that someday I would personally live the lyrics of the song.

I still sing Then I Met The Master but it is now delivered from a different point of view.

I have looked back to that night many times, wishing that I could start there again and create a more beautiful history the second time around. But I can't!

For the next three years I played at being a college boy while at the same time, traveling all over the southeastern states with The Songsmen.

By the close of my third year with The Songsmen, I had concluded that life as a single man was not going to be an enjoyable experience and I initiated a strong effort that I hoped would soon find me at the proverbial matrimonial altar.

On. October 19, 1963 my pursuit was rewarded. I found myself saying, "I do!" in response to the ministers cue as I made Betty Byrd, my college sweetheart, my wife.

You say, "What happened to college and The Songsmen?" The answer is simple, "I quit them both!"

No one, in either of our families, was delighted with me being a gospel singer and in order to achieve what they referred to as a normal life and motivated solely by their strong persuasion, I put my dream on a shelf and got me a regular job.

With music being the skill I possessed in the greatest abundance, I took a position as music director at a church in Akron, Ohio. My body and my brain were in the job but my heart sure wasn't. "You can lead a horse to water but you can't make him drink!"

Four months into my new church career the pastor became restless and asked to be transferred to a church in Newport News, Virginia. At his request, I moved with him.

Shortly after our arrival, a situation arose between two members of the congregation and their rivalry soon became a church wide battle.

I have never liked conflicts. Some would say I enjoy sticking my head in the sand! The truth is, I absolutely detest anything that interrupts my peaceful existence and will do anything to avoid a confrontation.

It only took a short while but I finally came to a point at which I declared to myself and to Betty, "If this is what Church and Christianity is all about, then they can have it! I'm through with the whole thing!"

Being grown and married now and having the luxury of being able to make my own choices, I chose to sever my relationship with both the church and church people.

Of all the bad choices I have made in life, that was probably my most destructive. It sent me forward on a road that, years later, would find me trying to end my own life.

Betty didn't share in my religious disenchantment but as a committed wife, she left the Atlantic seaboard with me and we relocated in Dallas, Texas. Her fears of the unknown were unimportant to me because I was determined to rebuild my own "field of dreams."

For numerous reasons but especially for the two lives she birthed into our family, I shall always be thankful to Betty for remaining the Christian lady that she was then and still is. She became the only cord of sanity attached to a life that would spin further and further from the center of life's true values.

God, in His divine sovereignty does not allow us the luxury of undoing actions from the past but for anyone who has ever wished to do so, I have great news!. God the Father through His only begotten Son, "Jesus The Christ," offers to us divine forgiveness and extends to us the opportunity to start "brand new!"

After searching thru every nook and cranny of society in search of building blocks for a new life, I have found that the most important are these! The assurance of strength thru "God's Divine Spirit" that I know lives inside me. The closeness of my own loving family. The support and prayers that emanate from my church family and finally, the warm friendship extended to me by my friends.

Upon these four foundation stones, "anyone" can create a "totally full-filled life."

Thank God for new beginnings. He truly has turned my scars into stars through His divine love and grace.

**"For all have sinned,
and come short of the glory of God." -Romans 3:23**

**"If we confess our sins, he is faithful and just to forgive us our sins,
and to cleanse us from all unrighteousness." -1 John 1:9**

"You can't grow corn from tomato seeds.
You get what you plant!"
-Donnie

CHAPTER TWELVE

THE SONG GOES ON

"**D**o you know of any quartet lookin' for a piano player or a lead singer?"

I was definitely through with church work and that was the question I asked my Uncle Jake when I called him in May of 1964. I was delighted to hear him say, "I sure do, me!"

J.D. was still with The Blackwood Brothers and had partnered with James Blackwood in the purchase of The Stamps Quartet Music and Printing Company in Dallas, Texas. Along with their acquisition came the company's performing name sake, the legendary Stamps Quartet.

Uncle Jake informed me that he and James were trying to organize a new group to promote the company. He told me that he had already considered asking me to be a part of the group but was reluctant to do so because he knew how my Daddy, his brother, felt about the wonderful world of gospel music.

It was soon settled that I was to become the manager, lead vocalist and pianist for his forthcoming group. In addition, I was to be the managing editor of Temple Music, the choral division of their parent company.

For the next year and a half I arranged choral works for Temple Music and sang four to five concerts a week with The Stamps Trio. I tell folks that we were the nation's "only" "Number Two" group at the time. Every other group was "Number One!"

In 1965, J.D. and James Blackwood divided some of their business assets with James becoming the owner of The

Blackwood Brothers and Uncle Jake receiving sole ownership of The Stamps Quartet. J.D. left the Blackwoods, joined the Stamps quartet and moved his entire operation to Nashville, Tennessee.

During late August of that year, the pianist for the Stamps resigned his position to become pastor of a Baptist Church in South Nashville and J.D. asked me to come join him as the new piano player for The Stamps Quartet. I readily agreed and soon I had my own bunk on my first quartet bus traveling with my musical idol, Uncle Jake!

I felt like I had died and gone to Heaven the first time I heard J.D. say, "How about a big welcome for the newest member of The Stamps Quartet, my nephew, Donnie Sumner!" It was on September 5, 1965 and I feel confident that the folks in Metropolis, Illinois had never seen a more graceful or longer bow than the one I gave that night. I was finally in the big league!

Not only was my new position a dream come true, it also felt great to be away from home and church again. My total responsibilities were riding, sleeping, eating and singing. The first year I was with the Stamps we did almost three hundred concerts and that didn't leave much time for me to be a husband. Waking up every morning in a new town, free to do just as I pleased seemed to me like a wonderful new way of life.

Over the next few years it would become increasingly more and more difficult for me to reconcile being a star three hundred days a year and having to empty trash at home the remaining sixty five.

Right after Thanksgiving that year, The Stamps were scheduled to make their first record with me. On the way to the studio that morning, the lead singer informed J.D. that he was leaving the group to enter the ministry with his preacher brothers. When we finally got set up in the studio to begin recording, I was the new lead vocalist!

47

I had always been accustomed to sitting at the piano and singing and the first night I did a live show with the Stamps I was rather motionless because I didn't know what to do with my arms. When we got back on the bus that night, Uncle Jake said to me, "Duck, ya sing great but ya gonna have to learn to move!" When I asked him what I should do he replied, "I don't know! Just make out like you're sweepin' the stage or swattin' flies or something'." He said, "What don't matter! Movin' is all that counts!" It took a while to refine the technique but I've been standing up, wavin' my arms and kickin' my legs ever since!

When I moved to lead singer, J.D. hired a teenager named Tony Brown to be our new pianist. To say that he was a humorous guy would be an understatement. The stage comedy that Tony and J.D. created together became a vital part of the success we enjoyed as a group. Tony was just beginning his career and I took it upon myself to "train him." I would have shown him a few more hot licks on the piano had I known that someday he would be the keyboard man for Elvis and would eventually rise to become Nashville's most respected record executive.

With the exception of J.D. everyone in the Stamps was less than a seasoned performer but Uncle Jake kept encouraging and training us. I know his task must have been difficult. If he had nerves, I'm sure we stayed on them!

Over the next few months, The Stamps enjoyed a fast rise in the industry and had become a major contender on the quartet circuit.

I still don't know when and where but as fortune would have it, Buck Owens was somehow exposed to our music. He was intrigued by J.D.'s low voice and invited The Stamps to do a song on his syndicated television show. The song we chose featured Uncle Jake on some extremely low notes. We really thought we had hit the big time for sure when the producer of the show contracted us to be special guest on each show for the remainder of the season.

From that time forward, J.D. and I frequently had a new golf partner! "Buck Owens!"

Success in life is kinda like "eatin' potato chips. You never get enough. There's always room for more!"

I enjoyed the thrill of success and I worked hard for it but one day the rain began to fall on my life and the wind started blowing hard against the structure I had built. It was then I discovered that success in itself was not sufficient enough to overcome the mess that followed.

"Except the Lord build the house,
they labor in vain that build it:" *-Psalm 127:1*

The only tower of my life that has remained standing at the end of every storm is the life that I have been able to construct founded on the sureness of "Jesus The Messiah!"

"Fear thou not; for I am with thee:
be not dismayed;
for I am thy God:
I will strengthen thee; yea, I will help thee;
yea, I will uphold thee
with the right hand of my righteousness." *-Isaiah 41:10*

The Stamps Trio always closed each program with a patriotic medley that began with, "My country 'tis of thee," etc. The opening night of our first tour in Canada, we started the song and the entire audience stood to their feet. I was delighted at receiving a standing ovation! I didn't know that the melody of our song was the same as their national anthem!

CHAPTER THIRTEEN
TOO MUCH CANDY

"Life is a bowl of cherries," some say. I thought it was too for a long time.

What could be better? My income was good. My popularity was rising and attention was coming my way in waves. Life was great!

On February 4, 1966, I was blessed with a son that we named, Jeffrey Dana.

I was snow bound in Boston, Massachusetts the morning I received the good news. The snow was almost waist deep in the city but I can tell you for sure, I've never had a warmer feeling! Ole tall and skinny me sure was a proud daddy!

Other quartets in the industry were being very kind to me and had begun recording a lot of my songs. In addition, J.D. and I were writing practically all of the tunes being recorded by The Stamps.

At the National Quartet Convention in 1969, I received the Gospel Music Association's, "Song of the Year - Dove Award" for my composition, "The Night Before Easter."

My second musical love is country music and I started trying my hand at writing country songs. Once again in '69 my writing efforts were rewarded. I was the recipient of two awards given each year by SESAC; "Writer Of The Year" and "Country Song Of The Year" for my work, "The Things That Matter." My ego was further elevated when my song, "The Things That Matter" was nominated by NARAS for a "Grammy Award" as "Country Song Of The Year."

My strongest competition was the song, "A Boy Named Sue" by Johnny Cash. When I get to Heaven, God is probably gonna say, "Donnie, why didn't you ever forgive Johnny for walking away with your Grammy trophy?"

I thought 1969 had been a good year but it was gonna be just as wonderful in 1970!

On the evening of March 6, 1970, my wife, Betty, placed another shining jewel into the crown of my living. I became father to the world's sweetest lady, my daughter, Robin Noelle!

At the time Robin was entering "her" world, I was trying to make "my" world bigger. I was on stage recording a live album with the Stamps Quartet.

To this day, I regret that my ambition caused me to miss two of the greatest events in my life. Namely, the births of my son and daughter, Jeff and Robin.

Along with all the glamor and attention I was experiencing, I was being drawn farther and farther from my family. The fun and follies were increasing and my family life was decreasing. If I had been my children I would have probably referred to me as Mr. Father because I sure wasn't around enough to be a Daddy! My only motivation had become my career!

In 1971, the Stamps joined the Elvis Presley show. Suddenly, "I" began to draw a much larger audience. Folks often asked me, "Did you really back-up Elvis?" I jokingly respond with, "No! He used to 'front' me!"

The big crowds, deafening applause, fancy hotels along with all the other perks of our association with Elvis acted upon me like a massive dose of drugs to a junkie! Some have said that, "I went crazy!"

I had been used to singing gospel songs in city

auditoriums and here I was singing "Do-Wah" and "Um-Pa-Pa" in places like Madison Square Garden and The Astrodome. The large church oriented crowds, to which I was accustomed, had turned into enormous gatherings of people screamin' their heads off.

The Stamps bus driver had quit a few months earlier and I had started doing most of our driving. I would sing until late at night and drive the bus until the middle of the next morning. Sleep was a luxury I wasn't enjoying much of and in order to make it through those long nights of driving I started taking uppers to keep me awake. I soon discovered that if I smoked a joint just before I lay down, sleep would come much easier and over a period of time I developed a constant routine of night time uppers and day time downers.

I was able to maintain that regimen for quite a while and at the time, things didn't appear to be too bad. Years later, I would look back to this period and realize that in my efforts to climb up the ladder of success, I was actually preparing myself for a descent that would eventually find me at the very bottom.

I was raised on the "gospel story" and I tried to over ride it's truth as a young adult but I can tell you something that is for sure; Once you have been exposed to the Gospel, you will never be able to out run it regardless of how hard you try!

All the songs I was singing with The Stamps were about God's love, His Grace and His Provision. The more lyrics I sang of this nature the deeper they would drive into my consciousness. It got to be, that every time I came off stage I felt like a dog. Here I was singing to folks about what they needed to do and what they needed to be, while at the same time, I was living a totally opposite lifestyle. I began to see myself as the biggest phony that ever stood in a pair of shoes.

Candy is sweet and wonderful but if you eat too much of it, you'll get sick and my life was beginning to consume too much candy! Life can be a bowl of cherries but it seemed my

52

bowl was turning into the pits!

It has been said of me, "He was at the wrong place at the wrong time!" I boldly proclaim to you that in God's sovereignty such a fact is impossible. You will always find Him to be at "the right place at the right time" God does not condone wrong but regardless of the situation He will constantly be by the side of a wrong doer with a hand of love reaching out to guide him toward a better place.

There is great reward in planting good seed in good ground. If a farmer plants fine seed he will enjoy a wonderful harvest because seeds reproduce in kind.

Much like the mythical, Johnny Appleseed, I did a lot of planting during my young life. Most of what I scattered were wild oats! It wasn't pleasant when harvest time came around but it sure was a wonderful event, the day I carried my ragged crop to the cross and laid it all at the feet of Jesus. He took the entire load and paid the receipt in full with forgiveness and grace. It sure felt good to have an empty wagon!

"Be not deceived; God is not mocked: for whatsoever a man soweth, that shall he also reap. For he that soweth to his flesh shall of the flesh reap corruption; but he that soweth to the Spirit shall of the Spirit reap life everlasting. "
-Galatians 6:7-8

"If we confess our sins, he is faithful and just to forgive us our sins,and to cleanse usfrom all unrighteousness." -1 John 1:9

"You can't sing with ya mouth full of chocolate.
It messes up the song!"
-Donnie

CHAPTER FOURTEEN
Elvis Is In The Building

Some folks know how to make an entrance. Others have the ability to make a grand entrance. Then there's the super grand entrance. Very few personalities have been able to master the latter but "Elvis did!"

It was about 7:00 P.M. on November 3, 1971, in Minneapolis, Minnesota at the Hilton Hotel. Elvis was scheduled to start a tour on November 5 and The Stamps, along with all the other members of the Elvis stage troupe, had been in the hotel ballroom since about 2:00 P.M. that afternoon waiting to begin the first of two six hour rehearsals. Needless to say, everyone in the room was excited as we anxiously awaited Elvis' arrival. This was to be my first tour with Elvis and I'm tellin' ya the truth, I couldn't hardly wait to get started!

All of us in the room were quite startled when the ballroom doors burst open like a car had hit them and Joe Esposito, Elvis' personal confidante, came thru the door hollering, "Ladies and gentlemen, Elvis is 'IN' the building!"

In line behind Joe, playfully pushing him out of the way, were Elvis' two chief bodyguards, Red West and Sonny West and then - there he was, - ELVIS!

Standing in the doorway dressed in his, now famous, blue suit with black laces holding the coat together, wearing a white shirt with his signatory high collar and frilly cuffs, sporting a blue velvet, Beal Street, hat and carrying a black cane with a big golden carved ornament on the top of it, Elvis was something to behold!

It was then I heard Elvis yell out, "What time does this 'two o'clock' session start?"

After taking his hat off and throwing it over to Sonny, he handed his cane to Red and then proceeded to shake the hand of each musician in the room. I wish I could express the feeling I had when Elvis stepped in front of me, reached out his hand to shake mine and said, "Hi Donnie, welcome to the family."

Family! That's what it really came to be. For the next six years I would come to know Elvis in ways that very few fellows ever had the privilege to experience.

Millions knew the name and experienced the persona of a superstar the world called, Elvis Presley but I have the joy-filled memory of having known Elvis as "my friend."

In my lifetime I have worked for numerous employers and I can truthfully say that I never developed a more deeply rooted friendship or ever had a greater respect for one's abilities than the brotherly bond and high regard which was to be created by my relationship with Elvis. He was a great "boss" and a "true friend."

During my years with Elvis, I would see more big cities, fly in more planes, stand before more people, shake more hands and receive more applause than I could ever have dreamed of.

The entire world knew Elvis as the "King of Rock" but I truly wish they all could have known the Elvis I call, "my friend!"

I have memories galore. Some of them I will share with any who wish to listen. Some of them I will hold sacred and only recall when Elvis and I, once again, have the opportunity to meet and reminisce together.

Elvis truly became my friend and I personally thought that I would never be able to create a more supportive, a longer lasting or a more certain friendship than the one that I enjoyed with my late friend, Elvis.

Then one day I met a loving man called, "Jesus The Christ" and in the years that have followed, I have come to know the power and strength of friendship in a fashion unlike anything I had ever known previously.

Should you be looking for the ultimate friend, I cannot recommend strongly enough, this man called, "Jesus The Lord!"

**"... lo, I am with you always,
even unto the end of the world." -Matthew 28:20**

**"... there is a friend that sticketh
closer than a brother." -Proverbs 18:24**

"A warm memory can turn raindrops into sunbeams!"
-Donnie

CHAPTER FIFTEEN
Don't Lose Your Marbles

"**H**e's lost his marbles!"

At times I've heard that said about me following something crazy I had just done or said and there was one occasion when I thought the same thing about myself!

It happened at the close of my first rehearsal with Elvis. In my opinion, that first rehearsal was a disaster. In the words of my friend, Joe Guercio, Elvis' orchestra conductor, "It was like watching a Russian movie with Chinese dialogue."

Elvis really liked the harmony and the extremely wide vocal range of The Stamps Quartet and because I had done all of the Stamps arranging, he asked me to be in charge of telling all the background vocalists what their particular parts were gonna be.

The Elvis background ensemble consisted of three ladies, The Sweet Inspirations, four guys, The Stamps Quartet plus J.D. and Kathy Westmoreland. Parts of the responsibility were easy, especially the clappin'.

On the older Elvis' songs we simply had to "Bop-Doo-Wah-Duh" or "Ooh and Ah" in what is referred to as block harmony. Of course, between these rhythmic words, there was a lot of "clappin'!" On these songs it was pretty much just, find a note and have fun.

No problem, so far!

For this new tour, several big production numbers had been added to accent Elvis' vocal skills. Songs such as, My

Way, You Gave Me A Mountain, American Trilogy and How Great Thou Art, among others. These type tunes required more precision than the "hang on and have a ball" songs.

Along with the "big songs" came "big problems!"

Elvis really liked the extremely high, lyrical obbligato's of Kathy Westmoreland. He also enjoyed the carefree style and rhythmic interpretations of The Sweet Inspirations.

Elvis had chosen The Stamps for our close harmony and because J.D. was his childhood hero.

In addition to the nine of us Charlie Hodge was on board singing all the duets with Elvis.

Each of our styles were totally different and we couldn't quite "git it together!" It was sorta like trying to push a rope!

To further aggravate the problem, The Stamps had two bass singers.

Earlier that year, J.D. had hired Richard Sterban as bass singer for The Stamps and Uncle Jake had become our featured soloist. When we joined Elvis, J.D. had only planned to travel along with the Stamps as our own Colonel Parker.

Elvis quickly and very definitely made it known that he wanted J.D. in the group so he could do, what he referred to as, "those B-59 bomber," zoom endings that was J.D.'s signatory vocal move and as always, when Elvis made a request, it became a swift reality and J.D. was suddenly part of the background vocals.

The lead singer in a vocal group always carries the melody of the song. In this case, Elvis was singing "all" of the melody lines. Every time I opened my mouth to sing I was on Elvis' part.

After about an hour of rehearsing, this is the plan I came up with.

For the majority of all ballads, I asked Kathy to sing the melody an octave above Myrna because Kathy could absolutely sing thru the roof and I told J.D. to sing an octave below Richard, which for J.D. was no problem at all.

For the most part, when singing harmonies together, The Sweets were to sing louder than The Stamps on the fast songs and vice-versa on the slower ballads and the gospel type tunes At that point, it pretty much began to level out and in a short time we had developed a rather nice sounding group.

As for me, my voice was jumpin' and dodgin' all night trying to avoid Elvis' lead vocal line but somehow, we managed to get to the end of the rehearsal without anyone noticing my inability to fit in.

At the close of the rehearsal Elvis went around giving each of us a moment of personal attention. During the time he was talking to me he asked, "How ya think it went, Donnie?"

I responded by assuring him that it was coming together and everyone was gittin' the hang of it. I concluded my response with, "That is, everybody 'cept me! Tryin' to find a part that won't get in your way is like tryin' to find a marble in bucket a' pearls!"

Elvis laughed that cute little laugh of his and replied, "Don't worry 'bout it! Just sing what ever ya want and when I point to ya, sing somethin' high."

The next night, just before we started our second rehearsal, Elvis' stepbrother, Ricky Stanley, came over to me and said, "The boss told me to give this to ya" and he handed me a nice little wooden box with a small golden clasp holding it shut.

I opened the clasp, lifted the lid and looked inside. The box contained a handful of marbles. On top of the collection there was a note in Elvis' handwriting. The note read, "You're here to stay, don't lose your marbles!"

When the tour was over I gave the marbles to my son, Jeff. Since then, I assume that Jeff either traded them for steelies or my daughter, Robin, secured them in the bottom of her fish bowl. At this point and I have no idea where they are hiding but with their disappearance, I can state for the record, "At least once in my life, I really did lose my marbles!"

Very often I find myself facing situations for which I have no answer.

I'm thankful that I have come to know one to whom I can go and talk over any problem that may arise.

The "Spirit of Jesus" The Christ, has often granted to me a peacefulness that my words are insufficient to describe.

"Casting all your care upon him;
for he careth for you." -1 Peter 5:7

"And the peace of God,
which passeth all understanding,
shall keep your hearts and minds
through Christ Jesus." -Philippians 4:7

"Success is climbing out of a hole without getting dirty!"
-Donnie

CHAPTER SIXTEEN
The Goose and The Tornado

Elvis loved to give gifts. He was one of the most giving men one could ever call their friend.

More than frequently, Elvis showered lavish gifts upon everyone that worked for him and I will always remember my first taste of his enormous generosity.

Right after our first tour with Elvis, The Stamps were scheduled to do an extended west coast tour and we were enjoying a short time off. During the break, Charlie Hodge called J.D. and told him that Elvis wanted us to come over and sing for him if we didn't mind. As usual, when Elvis invited you into his home, one "never minded!"

Early that same afternoon, The Stamps were en route to Graceland in our old gold and black bus that we referred to as, "The Golden Goose!"

Upon our arrival we were greeted by Charlie Hodge, who escorted us into the mansion.

When we entered the den we were met by Elvis, Red West, Sonny West, Mr. Vernon Presley, Joe Esposito and Ricky Stanley.

The room I am referring to as the den is now known as the Jungle Room and the name is fitting! The furniture, mostly of animal skin design had been arranged so that all of it faced the end wall. That particular wall had become a giant waterfall with a small lagoon at its base.

To say that the room made a statement would, itself, be

an under-statement. My first opinion of the room still remains the same today. It was Elvis' den and that fact alone made it "perfect."

We all sat around in the jungle room for a short while making small-talk.

It wasn't long before we all found ourselves in the living room singing gospel songs. As always, our "sing fest," became a quite lengthy session. We sang until about four o'clock in the morning,

Just before we closed out the sing-a-long, Joe Espisito came in and gave Elvis five velvet boxes.

I was surprised when he began to open them up, one at a time, and place the enclosed necklace around each of our necks. Man was that necklace pretty. It was an eighteen inch golden rope chain from which hung a medallion cast in eighteen carat gold. I can't express how I felt when he placed mine around my neck and said, "I'm glad you're in the family, Donnie!"

The symbol, I so proudly received, was to become the trademark for Elvis and all of his "family!" You've seen it I'm sure. It was the letters "TCB" resting on top of a lightening bolt. Elvis said it stood for, "Taking Care of Business!"

We sang a couple more songs after that and Elvis said he wanted to hear Sweet Sweet Spirit one more time. Elvis ended the request with, "Hey, J.D., before ya sing, I wanna see ya a'second." We started joking around with each other as Elvis and J.D. left the room.

In just a short time they both returned and as they started back into the den I noticed that J.D. was rather emotional and was puzzled as to why.

Just before we started singing Sweet Sweet Spirit, I saw Elvis put his arm around J.D.'s neck and I heard him say to J.D.,

"I love ya, my friend!"

I didn't know exactly what had taken place until we got back on the bus and J.D. shared this story.

"Elvis took me to the dining room and said, 'Anybody working for me' should have the best of everything and I want you to have the best bus in the business. Tomorrow I'm gonna have Daddy mail ya a check and I want 'cha to pick out the best bus ya can find and pay down on it. When it comes in, if you can't git financing on it, let me know and I'll pay the rest of it for ya."

If I had been J.D., I would have been a little weepy my own self, which I was a few years later and when he gave "me" a new bus.

Just before daylight, The Stamps finally found ourselves en route back to Nashville with J.D. sitting in the front jump seat. I might have been wrong but it seemed he was smilin' a little bigger than usual.

Wanna hear the epilogue?

We finished our west coast tour and stopped in Biloxi, Mississippi to pick up the bus J.D. had ordered. After taking possession of our brand new white bus, we headed home via Memphis so that Elvis could see it .

Once Elvis had seen the interior of our new "chariot" he wanted to drive it and drive it, he did!

Elvis cranked up the bus and started down his driveway toward Elvis Presley Boulevard.

At that time, most of the land directly in front of Graceland was an unfenced cow pasture and the average person would have turned either left or right onto Elvis Presley Boulevard. Not so with Elvis!

Elvis proceeded to drive across the highway, right out into the cow pasture and once he had safely cleared the street he floored the accelerator and hollered, "Hey, J.D.! Let's see what kind'a pick up she's got!"

I don't know if you've ever been on a bus speeding thru a cow pasture but I can assure you, from experience, it is more than rough!

After a few hard bounces, Elvis yelled over to J.D., "She's got the power of a tornado!"

From then on, that bus was known as "The White Tornado."

After saying, goodbye to Elvis, we continued our journey home with J.D. all alone in his new toy. The rest of us followed him aboard the "Goose" with me driving her to her final resting place.

Being at the end of a two vehicle procession, the only view I had was the back end of a white bus but I am certain that the on-coming traffic was witness to one of the biggest grins they had ever seen as J.D. stared back at them thru the windshield of his new "Tornado."

In my time I have both given and received a lot of gifts but I can honestly say that the greatest and most lasting gifts I have ever received came directly and usually unexpectedly from the gracious hand of "my Heavenly Father!"

His gifts always come with "no strings attached."

"Every good gift and every perfect gift is from above." -James 1:17a

"God so loved the world that He gave to us His only begotten Son." -John 3:16a

"An offering only becomes a gift when it is received!"
-Donnie

CHAPTER SEVENTEEN

Showdown At The E.P. Corral

Have you ever died? I did once. At least, I thought I did!

Elvis loved to play practical jokes on his friends and he sure did a number on me once.

The Stamps were enjoying our second engagement in Las Vegas with Elvis.

One morning about half way through the stay, Sonny West, the head of Elvis' security at the time, called my uncle J.D. and said he wanted the Stamps to join in a special security meeting prior to our first performance that evening.

When we all got to the meeting, Sonny announced that they had received an anonymous note from an irate fan stating the he was "gonna take Elvis down that night." Sonny went on giving directions in regard to handling the threat. He assigned each of us a section of the showroom to watch and that at no time during the show were we to take our eyes from our assigned section. During the show, if any male person stood up or moved in a suspicious manner, we were to shout out to Sonny or Red and point to the suspect.

Usually we never looked at anything but Elvis but during the first show that night I never lifted my eyes from my appointed section of the showroom.

To my relief, nothing happened during that performance but I was definitely not looking forward to the second show.

I had just returned to my room when Sonny called again

and said it was imperative that we all get together so I hurriedly proceeded to Elvis' suite.

Once assembled, Sonny again took charge and showed us a note from the alleged perpetrator stating that Elvis would be "dead before morning."

Red took the lead and started briefing us on a security procedure that involved a new seating arrangement that would have us encircling Elvis on stage. We were further instructed to surround Elvis on all sides in transit to and from the showroom.

Unnoticed during the briefing, Sonny had left the suite, changed clothes and was about to put the icing on the cake that Elvis had prepared for us.

Angling backward on the left side of the suite entrance there was a short hall. A full bar was against the wall just past this hallway entrance. Behind the wall there was a dining room that opens up into the living room at the far end of the bar.

Sonny had quietly re-entered the suite via the housekeeper's entrance and while Red held our undivided attention, Sonny came slipping down that hall dressed in all black and wearing a black ski mask.

Suddenly we heard a voice scream, "Elvis, take this!" The outburst was immediately followed by the extremely loud sound of three or four shots being fired from a handgun that the assassin was holding.

At the sound of the shots, Elvis and one of the hotel security guards did one of those movie type "I just got shot" moves and they both fell face down onto the floor as though they were mortally wounded. Red grabbed his stomach and fell down, in like manner, as though he too was seriously injured.

Bill Baize and Richard Sterban immediately jumped behind a long couch. Ed Enoch knocked over a big chair and was behind it trying desperately to reach the gun of the "not-so-dead" hotel security guard. Red, who knew that the guard's pistol was the only weapon in the room with live ammunition, was still acting critically wounded while, at the same time, trying to get to the guard's gun before Ed.

As soon as Elvis fell to the floor, my uncle J.D., a World War II veteran, immediately jumped on top of Elvis, covering his entire body with his own and just lay there. Elvis never forgot that J.D., unaware that he was being tricked, had put his own life on the line for him. The bond that was forged that night would never on this earth be broken.

When I heard shooting my first reaction was to get behind the bar as quickly as humanly possible. The ten feet between the bar and myself was covered in two giant steps with the third one becoming a leap that propelled me over the bar. Feeling safe behind the bar, I squatted down, looking along the wall toward the entrance to the dining room.

Unseen, Sonny had sneaked through the dining room and was on his way into the living room for one "final attempt."

As I sat there hiding, I saw a pistol slowly start to appear at the end of the wall to my left. When the pistol finally came into full view I realized it was being held by the "shooter."

Frightened to the point of nausea, I squatted there trying to find something I could use to knock the gun from the assailant's hand.

The only things under the counter were several large cans of tomato juice and orange juice.

With nothing else at my disposal and with "my death imminent," I grabbed a can of tomato juice with the intention of throwing it, as hard as I could, at the pistol I was looking at.

As soon as the can left my hand I knew that it was gonna

miss the gun by a country mile and without losing my momentum I jumped up, kept movin' and reached out to grab the gun.

Rather than the gun, I grabbed a slippery velvet jacket and the intensity of my lunge caused my hands to slide completely free of the sleeve and I fell backward onto the floor. That's when Sonny put the barrel of his pistol to my forehead and hollered, "You're dead!"

I might as well have been! I passed out colder than the proverbial cucumber.

I don't know how long it took but when I opened my eyes, the first things I saw were Sonny, dressed in all black and Elvis, laughing as hard as I had ever seen him laugh.

Needless to say, I did the second show that night with a queasy stomach but nothing really mattered except the fact that, "Elvis and I both were alive."

Tho not fearless in a physical sense, I now bravely face any situation which I encounter knowing that I am constantly under the watchful eyes of my "Heavenly father."

**For the eyes of the LORD
run to and fro throughout the whole earth,
to show himself strong in the behalf of them
whose heart is perfect toward him. -2 Chronicles 16:9**

Twenty four hours of every day I am under the protection of the greatest "bodyguard" in the entire universe.

**"And Jesus came and spake unto them, saying,
All power is given unto me
in heaven and in earth." -Matthew 28:18**

"Bravery is doing 'all you can'
when there's nothing else left for you to do!"
-Donnie

CHAPTER EIGHTEEN
GREENER PASTURES

In my travels, I have often seen large herds of grazing cattle. Occasionally I would see one of them hanging his head over the fence to stare at me as I passed.

If Daddy had seen it, he would probably have said, "He's just looking for greener pastures."

The poor cow didn't realize it but "If he jumped the fence, he would likely stumble in the ditch and if somehow he was able to cross the ditch, in all likely-hood he would get hit by a car!"

Much like that proverbial cow, I once jumped a fence and was eventually knocked to my knees.

In Elvis' 1972 documentary, "Elvis On Tour," The Stamps were privileged to be featured on several gospel songs. When the film premiered, we all attended and I got to see myself singing "The Lighthouse" with Elvis leaning over my shoulder listening intently. I watched it all the way through and when it ended I was still trying to figure out, how come my part was so short?

I have never gone around the world but "once upon a time" my face did.

In January of 1973, the Stamps were seen with Elvis in his world wide satellite special, "Aloha From Hawaii." Just prior to going on stage that night, I got too close to a broken tabletop in the dressing room and tore a big square completely out of my uniform's left leg. No seamstress was available and I only had a minute or two but I was lucky enough to have on a white suit and white shoes. With nothing else to do, I reached into my stage bag, got my liquid shoe polish out and painted that entire area of my leg "white."

If you saw the show and sometimes thought there was a fly on your screen. There wasn't! It was just "a hole in my britches."

Elvis worked a lot of dates but The Stamps continued doing gospel concerts when he was not in Las Vegas or on tour and with every gospel song I sang, the guilt feelings, that had begun earlier, got stronger and heavier.

Singing "Scooby-Doo-Wah" behind Elvis didn't seem to generate those same "guilty" emotions and I concluded that if I changed the kind of song I was singing they would go away completely.

Two months after Aloha From Hawaii I resigned my position in The Stamps Quartet and organized my own country group. We called ourselves, The Tennessee Rangers.

We were able to work a lot of country oriented nite spots around the Nashville area but our only claim to fame was being the "first" back-up artists to become regulars on Nashville's "Grand Ole Opry."

I got out of the Stamps Quartet but the Stamps never got out 'a me! J.D. Sumner and The Stamps "created me" and they will always be "a part of me."

Since then, I have come to realize, "it wasn't the song that was my problem, it was me!"

The Bible tells a story in Luke, chapter 15, about a young boy who jumped "his" fence in order to pursue a more fun filled life. The story relates his adventures and his ultimate demise. He wound up in a pig pen eating food with the pigs.

Some would surmise that the leading character in the narrative was the wayward boy but it wasn't. The "real" star of the work is portrayed only at the end when the boy decides that home was better and begins to head back to the "father's house." ***"And he arose, and came to his father."*** *-Luke 15:20a*

The story reaches its finale when the father meets the boy. ***"But when he was yet a great way off, his father saw him, ran, and fell on his neck, and kissed him.."*** *-Luke 15:20b*

It didn't matter how dirty he was, how messed up his life had become or how low he had stooped. With love, forgiveness and open arms, the father welcomed him back home.

Much like that young man, I too went in search of greener pastures but I never found them until "Jesus The Savior" opened His arms, welcomed me back home and became the living force in my life.

"I live; yet not I, but Christ liveth in me:
and the life which I now live in the flesh
I live by the faith of the Son of God, who loved me,
and gave himself for me. *-Galatians 2:20*

"Sometimes a situation is like bath water.
It's not all that hot once you get in it"
                                            -Donnie

CHAPTER NINETEEN
VOICE IS BORN

When I left The Stamps and organized The Tennessee Rangers we were the new kids on the block and nice engagements were hard to come by.

Just about the only requirement for most of the spots we were able to schedule was the ability to carry a melody and stand upright at the same time. Working a little club for a small fee was easy to book but my career had been built on the quartet circuit and I was accustomed to the loud response of the gospel fans. I quickly developed a dislike for the club circuit and set about to find another venue.

It was fortunate that my Uncle J.D. had become friends with Bob Whitaker, an executive at Opryland. Thru their combined efforts, The Rangers were able to perform several grand stand matinees at the Opryland Park. This was the side of "country" that I had hoped for. Performing good music before an appreciative audience

I was also blessed to have a personal friend in the country music industry by the name of Doyle Dykes. Doyle had been our guitarist when I was with The Stamps and we had developed a strong bond of friendship during that time. Doyle was a great Christian gentleman and was my first choice for guitarist when I organized The Rangers but his spiritual convictions would not allow him to share in our life style and I will always admire him for that. At this point, Doyle had become an established and highly respected musician on the Grand Ole Opry show.

Because of my friendship with Doyle, I took the liberty to use his name as my reference and became successful at finding favor with some of the Opry artists.

One of those folks was Carol Lee Cooper, daughter of the legendary Wilma Lee and Stoney Cooper duo. Carol Lee was one of Nashville's "first call" backup vocalist.

Carol and I joined forces and our combined talents became, Carol Lee and The Rangers.

Together, we were contracted as the first background vocalist to appear regularly on the Grand Ole Opry and as Carol Lee and The Rangers, we enjoyed the next few months singing "Oohs and Ahs" behind all the "rhinestone cowboys."

About a month after the show moved from Nashville's Ryman Auditorium to it's new Opry House, I got a call from Charlie Hodge who informed me that Elvis wanted my group to come to Vegas for a few days and that Elvis wanted me to do the "high notes" for his friend, Tom Jones who was having throat problems.

Vegas is very dry and unless you take special precautions, your voice will become very raspy and you experience what the singers there refer to as, Vegas throat.

When I was with Elvis as part of The Stamps, I would often hit the last big high note for Elvis. It was not because he couldn't hit the note, it was simply because he didn't want to.

Occasionally, he would attack an ending note and then point to me and I would sustain it for him so he could interact with a fan or do an impressive karate kata of some sort.

Following Charlie's call, I made the necessary arrangements to cover our absence from the Opry and soon thereafter, Sean, Tim and myself were en route to Las Vegas aboard Elvis' private jet.

For the next few days, three opry hillbillies got to play

"star" courtesy of our friend, Elvis.

The next weekend, both Elvis and Tom Jones ended their engagements and Elvis was hosting a closing night party in his suite at the Hilton. As Elvis' guests, The Rangers were included in the VIP list.

The late night had become early morning when I heard, "Hey Donnie!" I recognized Elvis' voice and I responded with, "Yes, Sir!"

I went over to where Elvis was and he said, "You remember that song, 'In The Sweet Bye and Bye' that you sang with The Stamps?" I answered him, "Yes, Sir!" Elvis smiled at me and said, "How 'bout singing it for me."

When Elvis smiles at you and asks you for a favor, how can you refuse? I said, "OK" and called for Sean and Tim to join me. We then got around Elvis' piano and began to sing.

Soon after we finished singing Elvis went into his bedroom. In just a bit, he came back into the living room, walked up to me, handed me a piece of bathroom tissue with writing on it and said, "Check this out and tell me what 'cha think!"

I took the folded tissue and began to read.

"I, Elvis Aaron Presley, agree to pay to Donnie Sumner, Sean Nielsen and Tim Baty, over the next twelve months, the sum total of XXXX dollars for their full time services to sing at my request, "In The Sweet Bye and Bye."

Once my eyes uncrossed, I said, "Are you kiddin' me?"

Elvis said, "No man! Y'all wanna be 'my' quartet?"

After a "split second" of deliberation, I said, "You bet 'cha!"

After the three of us had scribbled our signatures on the document, Elvis walked over to his dad, Mr. Vernon Presley, and said, "Well, Daddy, I finally got in 'a quartet!'"

Never in my wildest thoughts could I have ever suspected that a contract, opening the door to my highest dream, would have been penned in Elvis' bedroom on a piece of bathroom tissue.

The following week, Elvis took us all to his Hollywood home and shortly after our arrival there, Larry Geller, one of Elvis' close friends, came by the house to show Elvis his new book that had just been released entitled, The Voice.

Larry's book had a beautiful cover and after admiring the artwork a while, Elvis said, "Donnie, y'all ain't The Rangers no more! From now on y'all are, "Voice!"

Every night thereafter, until September of 1976, at some point during the evening we found ourselves around the piano singing old, slow gospel tunes for Elvis, as he would request them. Without exception, every sing-a-long included, "In The Sweet Bye and Bye." I recall one night when we sang the song eighteen times, back to back, all four verses.

That friend, is a lot of "sweet bye byes!"

"The Sweet Bye and Bye" is not just a series of lyrics in an old gospel tune. There really is a place of utopia existing in another, far removed dimension.

It's a gated community and each resident must sign the communal contract. There are no owner fee's and no insurance will ever be required.

I already have *"my"* suite in escrow and the closing was very simple.

I submit to you, it's a deal you can't afford to pass up.

"... Believe also in me. In my Father's house
are many mansions:
if it were not so, I would have told you.
I go to prepare a place for you.
And if I go and prepare a place for you,
I will come again, and receive you unto myself;
that where I am, there ye may be also." -John 14:1-3

"These things have I written unto you that believe
on the name of the Son of God; t
hat ye may know that ye have eternal life,
and that ye may believe
on the name of the Son of God." -1 John 5:13

"Always make sure you see water in the pool
before you dive in!"
-Donnie

CHAPTER TWENTY

THE VALUE OF A NAME

"Hi! My name's Donnie!" and the world says, "Donnie who?"

"Hi! I'm Elvis!" and the people start screaming!

The closest I ever came to the latter response is with the line, "Hello, I'm Donnie Sumner and I welcome you to the Elvis Presley Show!"

The difference is readily apparent. It's in the name.

I was always amazed at the reception received when lean, lanky, long-haired and sometimes misbehaved "lil' ole me" was afforded the privilege of associating my name with that of my friend, "Elvis."

A case in point!

During my years with Elvis, it was his habit, when at home in Memphis, to make Thursday nights his movie night. Every Thursday night we all found ourselves at the Memphian Theater enjoying a movie of Elvis' choice. It was usually very late because he would rent the entire facility after their normal hours of operation.

On one particular occasion, I had been away from the mansion since dark. In the pursuit of my "own" personal pleasures I had lost track of the time. I suddenly noticed that it was past the time I was supposed to meet the guys for our trip to the Memphian.

After assuring myself that I was totally irresponsible, I

asked myself, "Now what 'cha gonna do?"

I thereafter said to me, "Me, you better 'git there as quick as ya can!"

I immediately picked up the phone and called for a taxi.

Upon entering my "yellow and checkered" chariot, I promised the driver a "fifty dollar" tip if he could make the thirty minute trip in fifteen minutes or less and then I sat back to watch the cars and streetlights go whisking by my window.

In just a little over fifteen minutes I was stepping from my extremely swift and very expensive ride and walking toward the front entrance to the Memphian.

To my amazement the door was locked and I couldn't get in. That locked door really irritated me. After all, I was Donnie Sumner and I wanted in and I wanted in "now!"

During the major part of my years in the entertainment world, and then greatly escalating after joining the Elvis entourage, I had a tremendously over exaggerated opinion of my own self-worth. In those days, should one have occasion to open a dictionary to the word ego, they would have immediately observed my picture beside its definition.

Realizing that I, "Donnie Sumner," was being denied entrance by reason of a locked door and still highly excited by the wild ride I had just experienced, I started banging as loudly as I could on the door that stood in my way.

Previously that evening, I had really been "off duty" and was quite disheveled to say the least.

Standing there hammering on the door, dressed in "less than stylish attire" with my very long hair going in every direction and hollering, "Let me in," it's no wonder that when an employee of the Memphian finally came to the door, opened it up and saw me, he angrily said to me, "What 'cha' want?"

I started briskly pushing him aside and angrily said, "In and now!"

His response was to grab me by the arm and quickly assure me that my presence was not desired. Very gruffly he said to me, "You can't come in here. We're closed and having a private viewing."

At that point, anyone with any intelligence would have stopped due to the fact that the "grabber" was approximately twice the size of the "grabbee."

But not "Ole Duck." "Donnie Sumner didn't have to take that, off nobody!"

I reached up with my free arm and gave the gentleman a very firm shove.

I quickly reached down to grab the medallion that hung from a chain around my neck. I stuck my "TCB" up in the air like a cross holding back a vampire and defiantly hollered, "Back off dude! I'm with the Presley party!"

Bless his heart! It was like someone had poured a bucket of cold water over his head. He stopped in his tracks and politely said to me, "Yes, Sir! I didn't know!"

It's all in the name!

On another occasion, we were in Las Vegas a few days prior to Elvis' opening at the Hilton Hotel. That same week, Tom Jones was the main act at Caesar's Palace, just a short way from the Hilton.

Regardless of common belief, Tom and Elvis were very good friends and had great times together.

We had been in rehearsal all afternoon preparing for our up-coming opening night. When the session concluded, I assumed that we were through until late that night when we were to assemble again in Elvis' suite.

When Elvis got back to his suite there was nothing for him to do so he decided to go see the Tom Jones Show.

When Elvis party's, everybody party's.

Joe Espisito, Elvis' official family coordinator, called the guys and told them that everyone was going to Caesar's Palace to see the Tom Jones show.

When Joe called me I didn't particular want to leave at the moment and told him I would catch a cab and be over there in a little bit.

In a short time I was ready to make my departure and I went downstairs at the Hilton and had the doorman hail me a taxi.

As soon as I arrived at Caesar's, I went directly to the entrance of the showroom lounge.

There was a long line of people waiting for a table and like most patrons of the Vegas shows during that time period, they were all dressed in their finest apparel.

My attire was somewhat different from theirs. Dressed in a tank top shirt, blue jeans and Indian moccasins, I proceeded to make my way to the front of the line.

I finally found myself at the very head of the line, standing in front of two golden standards between which a wide purple rope was hanging and of course, "it was in my way."

As I reached down to unhook the small golden latch that held the rope to the standard, I felt a hand on my hand.

I looked up and it was the hand of a short, stout maitre-de, dressed in a black tuxedo.

As our eyes met he spoke to me in a distinct foreign accent and he said, "Sorry, sir! We have a 'dress code' here and even if you were properly attired you must 'wait in line'!"

Without a hint of a smile I said, "Negatory man! I'm with the Presley party!"

I find it amusing now but at the time, it did not strike me as funny when the maitre-de responded, "Yes sir! I'm sure and my sister is his wife."

I immediately reached down into my tank top and arrogantly retrieved my "TCB." I leaned forward as far as I could and held it defiantly right in front of his face and loudly said, "Does your sister have one of these?"

He smiled slightly and said, "Pardon me sir! Follow me!"

It really is "all in the name."

Time and events have changed my lifestyle since those times and I have become less Hilton and Caesar's oriented and have evolved into a more than frequent patron of a Waffle House or an interstate truck stop.

"Donnie who?"

"Elvis!" Now, that's a name!

There truly is power in a name of renown and I have discovered a name that is absolutely the most powerful name that has ever been spoken. I, personally have witnessed the name, "Jesus," being followed by blind folks seeing, crippled kids walking and deaf people hearing.

"Jesus!" Now, there's an awesome name!!

"And being found in fashion as a man, he humbled himself, and became obedient unto death, even the death of the cross. Wherefore God also hath highly exalted him, and given him a name which is above every name: That at the name of Jesus every knee should bow, of things in heaven, and things in earth, and things under the earth;" -Philippians 2:8-10

"A good name is like a glass of water.
The cleaner it is ... the better it is."
-Donnie

CHAPTER TWENTY ONE

THE PREACHER AND THE DOCTOR

Elvis enjoyed laughing and he would do anything for a good chuckle even if it required some serious money.

During one engagement at the Hilton Hotel in Vegas, a local pastor was doing a telethon on local T.V. in order to raise funds for a new church he wished to build. During my tenure with The Stamps, we had sung at this same preacher's church in another city.

His telethon was being broadcast from the Landmark Hotel which was directly across the street from the Hilton. Because he and J.D. were friends, the minister asked The Stamps to come over and sing on his telethon.

J.D.'s piano player had not come to Vegas for this engagement, so, Uncle Jake asked me to go along with them and do the piano work.

After singing for what seemed like a long time, the phone rang and the preacher announced, "I've got Mr. Elvis Presley on the line and he said that he would give $1,000.00 if J.D. would sing, 'Walk That Lonesome Road' and we did.

Elvis called twice within the next hour. During the first, he pledged $1000.00 if Bill Baize would sing, "When It's My Time" and called again assuring the pastor another $1,000.00 if I would do, "The Lighthouse."

We were singing by the hotel pool so it should have been no surprise when Elvis called back the fourth time and said He would give $1,000.00 if The Stamps would jump in the pool. As good sports, we all jumped into the pool. Just as I was about to hit the water, I heard Elvis' voice on the monitors saying, "Tell Donnie he ain't gotta jump, he's with Voice!"

Too late, I was already in the pool!

We were wet and chilled when we got back to the hotel. When we got upstairs we found Elvis and Dr. Nick waiting on us. Elvis gave each of us a robe to put on and Dr. Nick gave each of us a vitamin B-12 shot so that we didn't "come down with something."

During Elvis' first show the next night, he pointed to J.D. for a really low note and Uncle Jake flubbed it "big time." There was no reason for the bad note. He just "flat missed it!"

As we were going back up to the suite, Elvis jokingly said to J.D., "Great job on 'Amen' J.D.!"

There was absolutely nothing wrong with J.D. but he said, "It must have been the cold pool last night. I have some congestion in my lungs!"

J.D. should not have played sick because as soon as we got upstairs, Elvis called Dr. Ghanem, his Las Vegas throat specialist and shortly afterwards, J.D. found himself laying on Elvis' bed with Dr. Ghanem inserting tubes into his throat in an effort to relieve Uncle Jake of his non-existent congestion.

Suffice it to say, the Stamps never did another telethon nor did J.D. ever again create a phony excuse for any low notes he might have missed.

Elvis was a very giving and protective friend. He loved to take care of "his own." His joy was doing something special for those that he loved. If he was made aware of a need or even suspected one, Elvis would do all that was within his power to correct the situation.

Each of us have family and friends that we often desire to help but more often than not, either our power, knowledge or resource fails us.

I only know one person who can be at all places, at all times with all things. This singular person can be anything, to anyone, anytime and never diminish His strength or His reservoir of gifts.

His name is "Jesus The Christ" and His friendship comes easy. His door is never closed and He never goes to bed.

Twenty four hours of every day He is waiting, watching and wanting to help any and all who might wish to call upon His friendship.

"With God all things are possible." *-Matthew 19:26*

**"The eyes of the LORD run to and fro throughout the whole earth,
to shew himself strong."** *-2 Chronicles 16:9*

"Whosoever shall call upon the name of the Lord shall be saved." *-Romans 10:13*

"An open mouth is the biggest hole some folks will ever dig!"
-Donnie

CHAPTER TWENTY TWO
Don't Mention It

"If it ain't broke, don't fix it!"

My looks may not be perfect but please don't bring me discomfort in order to change 'em.

Not so with my friend, Elvis!

If there was an imperfection in your appearance and money could fix it, you better not mention it in the presence of Elvis or you might get a big surprise.

I have a large scar across the bridge of my nose, two oddly shaped and very large ears, along with a few other minor flaws but I will be eternally grateful that all of the above went "unnoticed" by Elvis during the times we spent together.

Let me tell you why!

Shortly after Voice joined Elvis, all the "Kings Men" went to Palm Springs, California for a few days of rest. The second night we were there, all the guys were sitting with Elvis in the living room kidding each other about who was the "best looking" and over a period of a few minutes each person had made a humorous comment about someone else in the group.

Because we were relatively new comers to the group, Sean Nielsen, Tim Baty and myself felt a little uneasy kidding the long standing members and therefore we had made no jesting overtures at this point.

Elvis, keenly aware, as he always was, realized that neither of us three had joined in with a comment and with a big laugh said, "I guess the only ones perfect in here is me and Voice!"

Sean giggled and replied, "I keep all mine covered up." Elvis asked, "What 'cha' coverin' up man? Ya look OK to me."

Sean answered him, "Well, my hair's a little thin on the top and I have to comb it up from the sides to cover it up."

Then pointing to his teeth, Sean said, "I've always had this tiny space here between my teeth so I just don't smile too big and not too many people notice it."

Not too much more was said regarding our individual looks and after a night of singing everybody went to bed.

The next morning, Elvis called Voice into the living room and as we came into the room Elvis said, "Hey guys, I want 'cha to meet my friend, Dr. Shapiro."

After the introductions were made and hands were shaken, Elvis pointed to a recliner adjacent to the couch and said to Sean, "Go over there and sit down. Dr. Shapiro's gonna' fix that space between ya teeth!"

Sean moved over to the chair, sat down and prepared himself as though he was about to watch a movie.

Dr. Shapiro brought out an old fashioned electric motor mounted on a piece of plywood and placed it on the coffee table. To that apparatus, he then attached a flexible arm that held a dental drill.

In just a few minutes Sean got up from the couch smiling and there for all the world to see were two beautiful caps, compliments of Elvis.

The end? Not on your life!

We had just finished lunch when the doorbell rang.

Red went to the door, opened it and invited the person standing there to, "Come on in!"

It was a short gentleman of oriental descent and I can neither pronounce nor spell his name but I can definitely tell you what he was and why he had come.

Elvis got up, shook the man's hand and shouted back toward us, "Hey, Sean! Come here! I got 'a surprise for ya. The Doc's here to give ya a hair transplant."

I was expecting Sean to loose his newly acquired caps but instead, he casually followed Elvis into the bedroom where the Doctor instructed him to lay down on the bed.

Elvis and the Doctor took a bed sheet, cut out a small circle in it and draped it over Sean's body with Sean's head centered inside the hole.

With us standing around the walls of the bedroom watching, the Doctor proceeded to remove one hundred small plugs of hair from the backside of Sean's head and insert them into one hundred small holes he had previously made in the top of his scalp.

Having successfully completed the procedure, the Doctor then wrapped Sean's entire head in a huge thick blanket of gauze. When Sean finally stood up he looked like Hollywood's "Invisible Man."

After that experience, if I ever looked in the mirror and saw something I didn't like, I immediately said to myself, "Don't mention it around Elvis!"

I love surprises only when they are good ones.

I have both given and received surprises in my time. Whether given or received, they all had either a negative or a positive response.

My "Heavenly Father" has been surprising me at some point during every day of my living since we first met.

The best part is this! Not one single gift from His hand of grace has ever brought pain into my life: He's never allowed sorrow nor regret to cloud the joy of any gift He has ever granted to me and may I also add; "He's not through surprising me yet!"

**" ... I am not ashamed: for I know whom I have believed,
and am persuaded that he is able
to keep that which I have committed
unto him ..." -II Timothy 1:12**

**"The blessing of the LORD, it maketh rich, and he addeth
no sorrow with it." -Proverbs 10:22**

"It takes both rain and sunshine to make a rainbow!"
-Donnie

92

CHAPTER TWENTY THREE

ARE YOU SINCERE

No singer allows a project to be released with off-pitch vocal notes.

No one except "Elvis," that is!

The "only" such work I know of that has ever been released was approved by Elvis and was done so for a purely personal and a very special reason.

On the evening we turned Elvis' Palm Springs living room into a surgical and dental clinic, Colonel Parker, "The Man," called Elvis and informed him that due to contractual agreements with RCA Records he *(Elvis)* had only a given numbers of days to have a project ready for release and further relayed to him that he must return to L.A. and "git into the studio and git 'a record out."

Although not privy to both ends of the conversation, I did hear Elvis' response. I heard him say into the phone, "Tell 'em, if they want my voice, they gonna have to come down here and git it."

With God, "all things" are possible!

With Colonel Parker, "most things" were possible!

For that reason, it should have been no surprise to anyone, when early the next morning, a huge tractor-trailer truck pulled up in front of Elvis' front door at his Palm Springs hide-a-way.

To the amazement of Elvis, three men jumped out of the

truck and began to unload equipment.

Within a short time, they had transformed Elvis' living room into a state of the art recording studio and Elvis was soon to begin the creation of his "Promised Land - Are You Sincere" project.

Having had no prior knowledge of the upcoming event, Elvis had not chosen a single song nor contracted a solitary musician.

Charlie Hodge, who had been placed in charge of these details by the Colonel the night before, had tried to schedule all the band members and get them to Palm Springs on a moments notice. Because most of them had prior commitments to various artists, Charlie was only successful at obtaining the services of James Burton, who arrived shortly after the "living room" studio had been prepared.

After we all got together in the living room, Elvis took a microphone, stood up on top of the coffee table said in a radio announcers voice, "Dearly beloved, we are gathered here today in the presence of these witnesses to make a record and I have one simple question to ask, 'What'n the heck we gonna' record?'"

As we did a lot of times, in response to his unique style of entertaining us guys, we had a big belly laugh.

Then with a more serious tone he asked, "Really, what we gonna' sing?" As though the "we" of the question truly mattered.

James Burton began to play some ole fashioned "rock-a-billy" licks on the guitar to which Elvis began to respond with those unique rhythmic sounds that only he was capable of rendering. Charlie Hodge joined in by playing drums on the back of his guitar and eventually Elvis broke into a version of "Promised Land."

That impromptu performance, after editing out all the trash and overdubbing some more instruments, became Elvis' next successful single.

After "Promised Land" and a couple of other standards were on tape, Elvis repeated a statement that my Uncle J.D. used to make when it was about time to shut down a living room sing-a long, "Well, if all minds and hearts are clear let's stand and be dismissed." Then Elvis ended the statement with, "I'm out 'a songs!"

I was playing the electric piano, Charlie was playing drums on the back of his guitar, James Burton was rockin' out on his guitar and Tim Baty, the baritone singer in Voice, was on acoustic guitar and for the most part we just jammed for a bit while Elvis got with Sonny West and Red West and tried to figure out what in the world he was going to put on tape.

Elvis hollered to me and said, "Hey, Donnie! Write down the words to 'Mr. Songman,' 'I Miss You,' 'I Never Stopped Thinking About You' and 'Help Me'!"

I responded by doing what I always did when I was asked to do something by Elvis. I did it!

These were some songs that my group Voice had often sung for Elvis in the living room. He liked them and decided to record them. I guess the real reason was, "he had run out of anything else to sing."

I was the writer of the first two, "Mr. Songman" and "I Miss You."

"I Never Stopped Thinking About You" was a song by Tim Baty, the baritone singer in Voice.

"Help Me" was a work given to Voice by my friend Larry Gatlin and Elvis, more than frequently, asked us to sing it for him.

This particular song, Help Me, was also one of my favorites and I always enjoyed singing it with Voice but after sharing in Elvis' recording of the song and after standing behind him hundreds of times on stage, listening as "he" sang it, I am totally convinced that the song was destined from the beginning to be his. It still thrills me when I hear it being played.

We had been making music since early in the afternoon and now it was very late in the post midnight hours. Everyone was tired and to say the least, silly.

We still needed one more song to complete the album and after some debate between Elvis, Red and Sonny they eventually came up with the song, "Are You Sincere."

Our little four piece band began the intro and Elvis ran through it a couple of times and then Elvis came up with the idea that he wanted Sean, the tenor of Voice, to do a short obbligato repeat line of the words, "Are You Sincere" at the end of the song, much like Kathy Westmoreland would have done, had she been available. Elvis thought Sean possessed one of the nicest lyric tenor voices he had ever heard and loved for Sean to sing songs for him that allowed Sean to exploit the unique quality of his soft tenor sounds.

As you have already been told, the day before this recording session, Sean had received Elvis' gift of cosmetic dentistry and a two hundred-plug hair transplant.

Being in a tremendous amount of pain and discomfort, Sean had tried to manage the pain by taking a few painkillers. Though still able to function, Sean was in no way capable of maximum performance.

As the music to the final cut came to a close, Sean stepped up to the mike and began his beautiful, Elvis-arranged, one line solo ending.

"Are you sin-" came out with exquisite clarity of both

tone and pitch but when the "-cere" was released, it came out of Sean's mouth at least a quarter of a tone flat.

Elvis immediately began to laugh hysterically at the note Sean had so miserably failed to correctly pitch.

After the rush of laughter from all of us had subsided, Sean with his gauze covered head and his pain killer numbed body approached Elvis and said, "I gotta' overdub that ending, boss! I really blew it!"

Elvis laughed and surprised everyone when he said to Sean, "That's the first time I ever heard 'you' miss a pitch and I want the whole world to hear it just to prove to 'em you can't sing as good as me!"

They erased Elvis' laughing seizure on the end of "Are You Sincere," but Sean's note remains flat to this day, thanks to Elvis.

If eternity has CD players, I suppose, that on occasion, Elvis still listens to "Are You Sincere" and has a big laugh.

I know for sure that, here on earth, I do!

I have found that "people aren't perfect" and I have further come to know that sometimes, "even good people often make big mistakes."

Along with all of my other life learned experiences, I now know that if, somewhere along the line, a wrong choice is made, it is possible for one to pick themselves up, dust themselves off and "keep on truckin'!"

I should know! I've done it lots of times! Wanna hear a secret? I probably will again!

"I count not myself to have (succeeded) but this one thing I do,
forgetting those things which are behind,
and reaching forth unto those things which are before,
I press toward the mark for the prize ..." -Philippians 3:13-14

"Mistakes are like footprints.
If you go anywhere you'll make at least one."
-Donnie

CHAPTER TWENTY FOUR
Paper Doll Daddy

I love the beauty of a blazing, open fireplace!

Therefore, it was no coincidence that one of my Elvis "house" duties was to maintain a glowing fire in the fireplace at all times, including the summer.

Elvis enjoyed using colored logs in his fireplace and the one in Hollywood was gigantic. On occasion, I have been known to put as many as ten, Dura flame logs on the grate at one time. Needless to say, the multi-colored flames were always a spectacle to see.

It was my normal routine to go into the living room before Elvis got there to make sure that the flames were in full color when he arrived. On this particular morning, I was about to enter the den when I heard voices coming from inside the room.

I had no idea who it was or what was going on but my observation that morning is a memory that I truly wish every fan of Elvis could have shared with me.

Elvis and Lisa Marie were sitting alone in the middle of the den floor.

Elvis had personally stoked the fire and it was already showering radiant colors.

Lisa Marie was dressed in a long nightshirt and Elvis was donned in a pair of dark blue silk pajamas with white accent stripes. He had not yet shaven and his hair was in extreme disarray. He was a mess to see but it will "always" be one of my most treasured memories of him.

They were surrounded by what appeared to be an abundance of little bits and pieces of paper.

Can I be so bold as to tell you what the "King of Rock," the "Idol of Millions" was doing that morning? He was "cuttin' out paper dolls!" The best part was when I noticed that he was using Lisa Marie's, "little plastic scissors!"

The "world" remembers, Elvis "The Star," Elvis "The King" and numerous other "Elvises" of their own choosing but when I recall "my" memories of Elvis, that of "the paper doll daddy" stands out as one of my fondest.

No one will ever be able to alter any of my remembrances and I have "nothing" negative to say about my friend, regardless of his human frailties! "He was a good, gracious and kind man!"

I know! I lived with him! I worked with Him! I buddied with Him!

Furthermore, I've been where very few have stood.

I have seen "Elvis, The Loving Daddy!"

Elvis was a great dad, just like my Daddy was to me,

From time to time, someone would say to Daddy, "Your love for Donnie can't be as strong as the kind I have for my child because he's adopted," My Dad's response would always be, "I know he's adopted but I'd die for him. Can you say anymore than that about the love you have for yours?"

Thank God for "loving, providing and protective "Fathers!"

Wow! I just remembered I have a really "super Father!" and I talk to Him everyday!

"(My) Father which art in heaven, Hallowed be thy name.
Thy kingdom come. Thy will be done,
as in heaven, so in earth. Give (me) day by day (my) daily bread.
And forgive (me my) sins;
for I also (have forgiven) every one that is indebted to (me).
And lead (me) not into temptation;
but deliver (me) from evil." -Luke 11:2-4

"A father's arm is strongest when
he is holding the hand of his child!"
-Donnie

CHAPTER TWENTY FIVE
HERE COMES 'DA SHERRIFF

"**S**top! Police,"

To the fleeing perpetrator, I guess it only appeared to be Elvis with his head sticking up thru the roof of a Mercedes limousine but it "really was the police." Never-the-less, in Hollywood nothing is out of the ordinary! Why stop?

I can't recall the exact day but I do remember the incident very well.

Elvis' home in Hollywood was a nice estate, surrounded by a stone fence. Included in the amenities was a large swimming pool with a fully equipped, two bedroom apartment that was sometimes used for guest housing.

Ricky Stanley and myself had chosen to sleep in the pool house after a long night of singing and when one is "sacked out" and enjoying a good sleep, their least anticipated event is "gittin' up!"

I guess Charlie Hodge didn't understand that!

Early that morning, He called and said "Elvis wants y'all up here ASAP!" In response to the call from Charlie, I got dressed and went back to the house to see what Elvis wanted.

When I got back to the main house, Elvis said He was "gonna take us all shoppin'."

I had shopped a lot in my time but never with Elvis and I was quite excited at the prospect.

Donned in his "wow" attire, Elvis, along with Voice, Ricky and Red, all piled into Elvis' limousine and proceeded down the drive and out thru the estate gate to "do the town!"

Shopping with Elvis has a couple of unusual characteristics, especially when done in a men's clothing store!

First of all, Elvis was no expert on sizes, materials or colors and his sales pitch was simple, "If it shines, it's mine!"

Secondly, if you pulled anything off the rack and looked at it, Elvis thought you wanted it and the item immediately went into the growing pile of soon-to-be-purchased garments.

When we were all inside the store, the manager locked the front doors. Within a relatively short period of time we had enough garments by the cash register to just about fill his sales quota for an entire month. We had enough genuine leather jackets, designer jeans and flamboyant shirts to clothe a small army.

Elvis seemed to be satisfied with our array of loot and he said to Red, "Pay for it!" Red pulled out a credit card, gave it to the owner and the sale was finalized. The gentleman handed Red the receipt and with a very "big" smile said, "Thank You!"

With the festivities all completed, we all filed out of the store, got back into the limousine and started home.

Elvis' limousine had a window between the drivers seat and the passenger area with some fold up seats with their backs against the partition. These extra seats would open up and accommodate passengers with them facing the rear of the automobile.

The main back seat faced forward and was wide enough to comfortably seat three or four adults. Some of the amenities included in the limo were personal storage compartments in four places, an intercom system, and a large retractable sun roof.

We all seated ourselves with Ricky and I in the jump seats, facing the rear and the others, along with Elvis, facing forward on the back seat. Elvis was sitting next to the window on his right side. The space between the seats, as-well-as each of our laps, were all filled with garment bags.

I have to confess, one of the gentlemen facing the rear was as excited as a kid at Christmas.

As excited as I was, I really didn't know how excited one could really become. Things were about to go from "shoppin' to shootin'!"

We were driving thru the residential area of Hollywood, just a short way from Elvis' home, when suddenly a small red sports car came speeding out of a driveway, right in front of Elvis' limousine.

In an effort to avoid the car, Elvis' driver slammed on the brakes. When he did, all of us were thrown into motion.

With the exception of the two heads that bumped the partition window, no particular damage was done.

None that is, except to Elvis!

When we came to that abrupt stop, Elvis was thrown forward into the lap of Ricky. It really startled Elvis and he tremendously disliked unpleasant startles.

Elvis pulled himself up, reached over and pushed the button that opened the sun roof and then stood up in the back seat. When he stuck his head thru the opening he saw the little red car and also realized that it was speeding up and getting away from us.

He ducked back inside the car and hollered to the driver,

"Catch that car!" At the same time he reached over to a compartment in the right hand door and pulled out a gun with a barrel that looked as long as my arm. With the gun in his hand, he again put his feet on the back seat and stood up thru the sun roof with about half his body sticking thru the opening.

You must remember, we had just been shopping and Elvis was dressed in his full "Memphis - Beale Street" regalia. His riding attire included a wide brimmed hat, a short cape, a bouffant shirt and sun glasses.

Elvis' hat was the first casualty of the moment. When Elvis' head hit open air again, his hat flew off and has never been seen since. The draft from inside the car pulled his cape up thru the opening and it began to trail behind Elvis like a flag in a hard blowing wind.

If the guy driving the car in front of us had taken the time to look in his rear view mirror, it would probably have appeared to be Snoopy standing on top of a white car.

Hang on boys and girls! It gets better!

Elvis was an honorary member of numerous police forces in the United States. In his home, he had an entire bag full of genuine police badges and several of them were decorated with a precious stone.

I don't know if it was the shine of the badges or a childhood fantasy but I do know that Elvis loved to look at them and that he was mighty proud of 'em.

Never-the less, immediately upon "gittin' in 'da wind," Elvis, as if the little red car had ears, yelled out, "Stop! Police!"

Speeding thru "snob hill," we must have looked like the Keystone Cops when Elvis pointed his gun upward and fired a round.

Elvis' limo did not have nearly as much acceleration as the other car and it was certain we weren't gonna be able to catch up to the fleeing car so Elvis lowered himself back into the car, plopped down in his seat and didn't say a word until later that night.

It was an exciting shopping trip and we had a limo full of shopping bags but for the remainder of the journey back to Elvis' estate the limo's remaining cargo, one embarrassed driver, one long haired step-brother, one concerned bodyguard, three frightened musicians and one "silent" superstar - all remained extremely inactive.

The home of Rock Hudson was on the "high-speed-chase street" and after Rock's death, his estate was purchased by new owners.

If, on some warm afternoon, the new tenants should be walking around his or her beautiful estate and notice a small hole in one of their trees, they just might try to get a little closer to determine what had caused it.

If that person was a thorough investigator, he or she just might retrieve a long lost bit of "metallic memorabilia" left there by the late Elvis Presley.

In all probability the recipient of the treasure would have no idea as to the worth of the find and would probably just simply say to them self, "I wonder how in the world this bullet got into my tree!"

I can honestly say that Elvis was one the most generous persons one could ever hope to meet. I never asked him for a single thing but was the recipient of many. I like to think that anything I might have asked for, Elvis would have done it for me if it was possible.

I have come to know one "Jesus The Christ" who can be all places at all times and be all things to all people. I have discovered that if I ask Him for it - it's on the way.

"And all things, whatsoever ye shall ask in prayer, believing, ye shall receive. -Matthew 21:22

"... ask, and ye shall receive, that your joy may be full." - John 16:24

"You can't hit the moon with a B.B. gun but you can come closer than someone who's not shootin' at all.
-Donnie

CHAPTER TWENTY SIX
Kung Fu - R - Us

Elvis and I had a lot of opposites!

He was handsome, I wasn't. He was rich, I wasn't. He was famous, I wasn't.

He knew Karate and I didn't.

I always dreamed of being handsome, rich and famous but never at any time did I aspire for the strenuous discipline required to become proficient in the art of self-defense. Therefore, I became quite concerned when Elvis announced to Voice. that he was going to teach us the art of Karate.

We were in Palm Springs and all of us in Voice were swimming in the kings pool when Charlie Hodge stepped onto the patio and announced, "The Boss wants to see y'all!"

We climbed out of the pool, grabbed our towels, dried a little and proceeded into the house.

When we got inside the house, Elvis was standing in the middle of the living room dressed in his karate uniform and it was then that Elvis made the announcement that we were about to begin training.

Elvis lined the three of us up and began to demonstrate various short katas, a series of moves resembling ballet movements. He then had us to try duplicating them. I wasn't doing too badly until they got down to kicking.

Elvis made a mark on the wall for us to aim at and each of us were to try kicking the spot. Sean was adequate. Tim was great! "Ole Donnie," well, he never could get his foot higher than his waist!

When it came my turn to try, my effort fell short of the goal. I completely lost my balance and fell backwards, flat'a my back onto the floor.

Elvis started laughing, jumped on me and began to act like he was giving me CPR.

It didn't take Elvis long to determine a truth, "You can't teach an unwilling dog a difficult trick!"

After we had worked up a good sweat Elvis called it a day and told each of us to create a personal kata for the next day. After much thought that night, this is the "D.H.S. self-protection kata" that I demonstrated to Elvis the next morning.

You brace yourself in a defensive stance. Slowly draw your left foot backward approximately two feet and follow that by slowly moving your right foot backward the same distance letting both feet touch. After repeating this move three to four times, you turn your body one hundred eighty degrees and "run like crazy!"

With that, Elvis fell to his knees and started laughin' really hard.

I always enjoyed making Elvis laugh.

God must like to laugh Himself 'cause He made monkeys and "me!"

I have cried thousands of tears in my "New Life" but through all of them, I can report that by the help of "My Heavenly Father" I have been granted the joy of a strengthening laugh on millions of occasions.

Good news boys and girls! I'm expecting a lot more laughs to come my way!

"... eat the fat, and drink the sweet ... for the joy of the LORD is your strength." -Nehemiah 8:10

"Just like it raises the corners of your mouth,
a good laugh will always lift your spirit!"
-Donnie

CHAPTER TWENTY SEVEN
THE TEACHER

I have a very short attention span!

Unless I am really interested in a subject, it usually receives only limited concentration on my part.

Having tried to avoid educational pursuits for quite a while, I was not overly excited when Elvis came into the living room one morning and announced that he was gonna teach Voice the art of meditation.

Until this time, my idea of meditation was laying back in a leather recliner with my eyes shut.

That morning found all the members of Voice in the middle of the Elvis' living room, sitting in a circle with Elvis in the middle.

He had given each of us a golden necklace with a jade ornament. We were told to place it around the top of our heads with the jade ornament resting on our foreheads between our eyebrows.

Elvis then had us sit on small pillows and take our legs, bend them at the knees and place each ankle on its opposite thigh. It was only a little uncomfortable at the time but at my present age, it "hurts" just to think about it.

After getting in position, we all joined hands, closed our eyes and in a monotone voice, Elvis began verbalizing a mantra.

He then began instructing us on how to use the word "ohm" and certain breathing techniques to acquire a state of total relaxation.

After several minutes of vocal and breathing exercises, Elvis began to explain the value of colors and their ability to create a desired result. For instance, blue for tranquility, green for healing, yellow for happiness etc. We were to practice visualizing friends and family members surrounded by a specific color.

I sat there repeating the mantra, "Christ Light, Christ Peace, Christ love. Oooooooohm ...Christ Light, Christ Peace, etc." over and over again.

I can't speak for the other guys but my only experience during this training session was a case of very sore knees.

Apparently my brain became more relaxed than my body because during a moment of silence I unexpectedly yawned and Elvis responded with, "Scuze me! Will ya please!" To which everyone began to laugh, especially, Elvis.

Sensing that we had lost our inspiration, Elvis reached down and picked up three small black books and gave one to each of us. It was a book on meditation entitled, "The Impersonal Life."

Inside the cover of each book, Elvis had written a personal comment. The note to me read, "To Donnie: May 'The Light' give you warmth, protection and direction until you reach 'Home.' Friends forever, Elvis."

Later that night, Elvis said he wanted to talk to me. I was quite uncertain as to what was about to happen but I followed him into his bedroom and together we sat down on the bed.

Within a short time Elvis began to talk about meditation and his need to join with someone from whom he could draw spiritual reinforcement for his weakening inward man.

During our time together that evening he never really shared with me the inward battle that he was having but I determined from some of the comments that he made, that it was centered around his relationship with Priscilla and that he was seriously troubled about what ever his unstated thoughts were. At one point he said, "Man, I think I'm goin' off my rocker! It feels like I'm losing my marbles!"

To honor his request and really believing, at the time, it would accomplish a positive reaction in his "psyche," we both joined hands with his right hand in my left hand.

For a considerable period we just sat there breathing slowly.

Some time later, with no other words spoken and with Elvis still in silence, I got up and quietly left him alone in his bedroom.

The next day, while shopping with Ricky in Palm Springs, I remembered a past moment with Elvis and at the same time I thought about the previous night. It was then that I had what I thought was a "cool" idea.

I found a little souvenir shop, went in and bought a very large and beautiful, crystal clear, aqua colored marble that cost about five dollars.

That night when we all got back together with Elvis, I waited until I could get to Elvis in a private moment and when the opportunity did arrive, I quietly said to him, "Boss! Ya remember how you said you felt last night?" He nodded his head and made a soft, "Um-huh" sound. I reached out with my closed hand and put into his hand the marble I had bought earlier that day, and I said to him, "Put this in ya pocket and hang tight. You 'da man and with this in ya pocket, you ain't never gonna lose 'em!" He smiled and we returned to the evening festivities.

If I could snap my fingers and bring into existence all the things that I might wish for at this point in my life, there's one thing I would snap into reality.

I would snap Elvis into today and at the age we would both be, it would probably be quite enjoyable for both of us to find those glass orbs, from a time once lived, "suddenly" back in our possession again.

I like to think that, together, we just might duck out the back door of Graceland, run down into the horse pasture, find ourselves a little sandy spot, squat down and shoot a game with the "marbles that we both lost" once upon a "real" long ago.

Although I practiced the art of color transference for a while, I must admit, that to date, I have not received any confirmations of receipt.

On the other hand, I have experienced many great successes when I called forth the promised provisions granted to me by "My Heavenly Father" and transmit His enormous powers in the name of, "His Only Begotten Son," "Jesus The Christ!"

With my own eyes and ears I have witnessed the healing, peace, strength and direction that can come with the speaking of "that Name!"

It's easy to do! There's no particular position or mantra required. All you have to do is tell "The Father" what you need and ask Him for it!

**"Whereby are given unto us
exceeding great and precious promises:"** *-II Peter 1:4*

"Every good gift and every perfect gift is from above, and cometh down from the Father of lights, with whom is no variableness, neither shadow of turning." *-James 1:17*

**"And all things, whatsoever ye shall ask in prayer, believing,
ye shall receive."** *-Matthew 21:22*

"Choose to be happy! You can't wring your hands
and roll up your sleeves at the same time!"
                                    -Donnie

CHAPTER TWENTY EIGHT
WHAT WAS ELVIS LIKE

I sent out a questionnaire to all of my friends around the world and asked them to submit a one line question they might wish for me to address in my memoirs. I was surprised by the number of emails I received in return.

I was further surprised when four questions covered more than ninety percent of the responses. One of these was, "What was Elvis like?" I frequently respond to this question in a comical manner by saying, "He was the best looking, most talented and richest 'cotton picker' I ever met!"

In truth, Elvis was a multi-faceted individual and each element in his world was quite unique.

"Elvis, the superstar" was an entertainers role model!

He was a man who had risen to the zenith of the entertainment business from a life of poverty. Unlike most stars I have known, in the process of "becoming famous" he never forgot those who were with him at the beginning. His childhood buddies were some of his closest associates. To those of us who knew him best, he was not only a star, he was our friend and a buddy. He knew what he wanted on stage and we tried to give it to him. He was not demanding but we reacted to his wishes freely. We respected his position as a "superstar" and he most graciously recognized our supportive roles.

Because of my friendship with Elvis I have had the privilege of being in the company of numerous big stars and in my opinion no one ever played the "star role" with greater poise and grace than Elvis did. Whether it was on stage, in his home, hanging around with guys or being a boss, Elvis was always kind, considerate and gracious to all of us. To each of us, he was definitely "number one" but it was "not" by his "demand." Respect was our personal choice and it was freely given. We all admired him for "what" he was and not because of "who" he was.

"Elvis, the singer" was a great vocalist?

I have both studied and taught voice. I have also had the opportunity to teach vocal pedagogy which is simply teaching teachers and I can assure you that Elvis was a great singer. His singing voice was not all that mature when he began his career but thru the years, Elvis perfected all of the qualities necessary to achieve the status of both "great vocalist" and "excellent performer."

The average singing range is about one and a half octaves. Elvis had a singing range of nearly three octaves. The breath control of a singer determines the volume of their tones and the length with which they can sustain them. When it was needed, Elvis' voice could be extra ordinarily loud and he could hold a note longer than anyone I have ever known.

All singers strive for clarity of diction and perfection of communication. Very few artists acquire both with excellence but Elvis did. You could understand every word he sang and when he was finished you understood the entire message of the song. In the music industry we call this "milking a song" and Elvis had this ability in great quantity.

No one gets excited when a singer is motionless and the art of "stage presence" is something rather unheard of in today's music industry. Most everything is choreographed and done in unison with others. There is very little action which is uniquely personal. Elvis commanded the stage when he performed. Everything he did was unique to him alone. Whether it was an eye movement, arm thrust or leg motion it was "definitely Elvis!" Elvis was definitely a skilled vocalist and a superlative performer.

"Elvis, the Man" was the side of Elvis that we all loved the most.

Once the lights went out, the fans were gone and the jump suit was in the closet, my favorite Elvis came into view. Wearing relaxed clothes, sporting an imperfect hair do, simply laying back on the coach with his feet on the coffee table and laughing. That's the Elvis I most often recall.

When all of the accolades have been voiced and when all the compliments have been noted, the bottom line becomes a simple statement.

Elvis was, above all other things, a "kind and considerate friend!"

Everyone needs a friend and I have found a great one!

He has become known to me as "Lord Of My Life!"

In Him I have found perfection, integrity and kindness unlike anyone who that has ever come into my life.

**"All the promises of God in him are yea,
and in him Amen."** *-2 Corinthians 1:20*

"As for God, his way is perfect." *-Psalm 18:30*

**"Come ... casting all your care upon him;
for he careth for you."** *-1 Peter 5:7*

"It takes more than whiskers to make a man.
Nothing does the trick like a loving heart
and a helping hand!"
-Donnie

CHAPTER TWENTY NINE
THE GIFT

One question I received several times was, "How do you think Elvis got so famous?" To answer the question requires more than a passing comment.

May I start with this statement. Without exception, everyone is born into this world with a God given talent. Some might refer to this talent as a "gift." Regardless of the word by which it is called, every person is granted one and it comes in many forms. To some it might be a technical skill, while others may be gifted in numbers, science or music etc. I always said my Momma's gift was "Divine Spoons" because she sure could cook.

> *"Having then gifts differing according to the grace that is given to us." -Romans 12:6*
>
> *"Every man hath his proper gift of God,*
> *one after this manner,*
> *and another after that." -1 Corinthians 7:7*
>
> *"Unto every one of us is given grace*
> *according to the measure of the gift of Christ." -Ephesians 4:7*
>
> *"Every good gift and every perfect gift*
> *is from above."-James 1:17a*

We spend our lives trying to attain success but only find it when we discover the "divine gift" that the creator has granted us and when we focus our efforts toward maximizing that particular talent. Various endeavors are fine, hobbies are fine but success comes when you remain focused on the one thing that you do best. You will never be able to fit a square peg into a round hole.

> *"A double minded man is unstable in all his ways."* -James 1:8
>
> *"Neglect not the gift that is in thee."* -1 Timothy 4:14
>
> *"I press toward the mark for the prize*
> *of the high calling of God in Christ Jesus."* -Philippians 3:14

When one utilizes and maximizes the unique talent that the Father that has given to him or her, the gift, in and of itself, has the power to help achieve success in the effort.

> *"A man's gift maketh room for him,*
> *and bringeth him before great men."* -Proverbs 18:16
>
> *"Every man should ... enjoy the good of all his labour,*
> *it is the gift of God."* -Ecclesiastes 3:13

God does not change his mind, even if one never recognizes the nature of their gift or if they comprehend it and point the gift in a direction opposite to His original intent. Once given, it always remains and nothing can remove it from your living.

> *"The gifts and calling of God*
> *are without repentance."* -Romans 11:29
>
> *"And cometh down from the Father of lights,*
> *with whom is no variableness,*
> *neither shadow of turning."* -James 1:17b

All music comes from the heart of God and was intended to bring him pleasure and glory. The highest angel in Heaven was a musician and his only responsibility was to make God's heart joyful with his beauty and the sound of his music.

> *"Thus saith the Lord God; thou sealest up the sum, full of wisdom, and perfect in beauty.*
> *Thou hast been in the garden of God;*
> *every precious stone was thy covering,*
> *the sardius, topaz, and the diamond, the beryl, the onyx,*
> *and the jasper, the sapphire, the emerald,*
> *and the carbuncle, and gold:*
> *The workmanship of thy tabrets and of thy pipes*
> *was prepared in thee*
> *in the day that thou wast created." -Ezekiel 28:13*

Elvis had the gift of music and this particular gift has a unique way of attracting attention to itself and it will invariably effect the emotions of anyone exposed to it's delivery. Even though the gift that he was given was not always pointed toward "the giver" it never lost any of it's power.

In my opinion, it is no coincidence that the only albums Elvis ever received a Grammy award for were, "How Great Thou Art" 1967, "He Touched Me" 1972 and "Best Inspirational Performance" 1974.

> *"So shall my word be that goeth forth out of my mouth: it shall not return unto me void, but it shall accomplish that which I please,*
> *and it shall prosper*
> *in the thing whereto I sent it." -Isaiah 55:11*

Elvis determined his gift early in life and was never side tracked by anything that would draw him away from his musical dream. He pursued it constantly, worked for it untiringly, refined it to perfection and great success was his reward.

Most folks attribute Elvis' fame to Colonel Parker because of his management skills and promotional abilities. On the other hand, I have a different perspective.

I am persuaded to believe that before the worlds were ever formed, the heart of God ordained and anointed Elvis to be a "Psalmist' much like little David was to King Saul, as recorded in, *-I Samuel 16:23.*

I further believe that this "Davidic Anointing" shadowed Elvis all the days of His living. I am satisfied in knowing that neither the form by which he presented it nor the places in which he chose to exposed it mattered. I am convinced that the "divine anointing" we perceived as his "musical gift," in and of itself was the single most important ingredient to Elvis' successful career.

My final comment would be this; "According to His promise, "The Father of all gifts" blessed and rewarded Elvis' efforts with world wide acclaim.

"He that gathereth by labour shall increase." -Proverbs 13:11

"The Lord shall increase you more and more." -Psalm 115:14

"I have planted, Apollos watered;
but God gave the increase." -1 Corinthians 3:6

"A gift from God is much like one's head,
you don't have to use it but you can't get rid of it!"
-Donnie

CHAPTER THIRTY
DID ELVIS DO DRUGS

Questions in regard to Elvis and drugs was the second largest group of inquiries I received in response to my survey and is a subject I truly wish no one had asked about.

At the onset of my response, may I say, "I did" and lots of them!

When someone was trying to persuade me to quit doing drugs, I often said in jest, "everybody needs a crutch!"

The reality is, everyone "does need" something with which they are able to reinforce the weakness of their own human frailties.

In the secular world, some resort to social power, some to money, others to reckless living and the list continues. Even a faithful believer relies on the inner strength of Christ to make them an over comer in life. No one is "perpetually strength sufficient" in "their own power."

I, personally, found a powerful illusion of myself hiding within the drug culture.

Never is the need for this reinforcement greater than when a person rises to a place of high public visibility.

The press proclaims you to be greater than life itself and each morning you have to look into the mirror and view the image of one whose short-comings you know all too well. Regardless of what others might see, "you can't hide from yourself!"

I have fallen prey to this liability frequently but I have

never experienced it in the same fashion as my friend, Elvis. I was just a back up singer. He was a "superstar."

The press called Elvis, "The King of Rock and Roll" but he could never reconcile the phrase with the fact that he was just a poor boy from Mississippi that had gotten very lucky. Ole "E" was simply "a good ole boy" and that was easy to live with. On the other hand, to maintain the persona of "Elvis" was a monumental task.

With those thoughts as a preface and truly knowing that it did not make my friend a bad person, I "regretfully" have to respond to your question with, "Yes, Elvis often used various substances and further more, I did them with him!" In addition I make a strong distinction between the phrases "drug user" and "drug addict!" My friend, Elvis was a drug user but I became a drug addict.

Elvis and I spent numerous occasions in revelry together laughing at ourselves. Things seemed to be funnier during these "high" moments than they really were. After all, the primary goal of this choice was for enjoyment and at the time, we believed that we were having a lot of fun.

A some point we would have to call it a night, go our separate ways and try to find some comfort in sleep. Finding it impossible to sleep after such an evening, Elvis probably did the same thing I did and take some form of sleep aid in order to relax and go to sleep.

It really was a fast and furious life style and I don't know how we maintained it.

Friends often asked if Elvis died of a drug overdose and the answer is definitely, "No!"

It was simply the "effects" of a "life stye" that finally had the last word.

On the morning of August 16, 1977, Elvis was headin'
back to bed, and his body said, "You can go get in that bed if
you wanna but 'this' is where 'I'm' gonna 'lay down'!"

Then, for the first time in many years, Elvis was no
longer captive to press reviews and no longer had to be "what
someone else said he was!

*At this point in my life, I am not overly concerned with
"who I am" or "what I am."*

*You see, I now have an unseen power living inside of
me that enables me to do things and think things that far
supersede the abilities that "ole Donnie" might possess
within his human personae.*

*I have found that the true source of "life
reinforcement" and the greatest resource of "right thinking"
that one can ever locate was found and received by me when I
allowed "Jesus The Christ" to become the director of my
living!"*

**"... I live; yet not I, but Christ liveth in me:
and the life which I now live in the flesh
I live by the faith of the Son of God,
who loved me, and gave himself for me." -Galatians 2:20**

**"I can do all things through Christ
which strengtheneth me" -Philippians 4:13**

"Looking at the road ahead is much safer than
staring in the rear view mirror!"
-Donnie

CHAPTER THIRTY ONE

Was Elvis A Christian

"**W**as Elvis a Christian?"

Overwhelmingly, that was the question most frequently asked in regard to my friend, Elvis.

In response, certain facts must be presupposed.

First, nobody can answer with certainty, any question regarding another person's relationship with God. We must depend entirely upon their personal affirmation and thereafter must suppose that declaration to be the fact.

Secondly, with the absence one's personal confirmation, it is never appropriate for a person to judge the spiritual integrity of another individual. None of us have the knowledge of God.

It is the nature of human reasoning for one to observe the life style and actions committed by another and thereby establish an opinion based upon personal persuasions in regard to denominational beliefs and their corresponding code of conduct. May I say, "that is only a perceived interpretation and may or may not be an established truth."

The fact is, no one has the duty, the right nor the luxury to answer such a question.

Never-the-less, my first response would be, "I don't know." I would then proceed with an explanation of my short answer in an effort to not appear evasive or cold-hearted.

I only had a personal acquaintance with Elvis for a brief

six years. Compared to the forty-two years of his living, that is only a short span of time.

A black minister in Mississippi publicly declared that he had the opportunity to baptize Elvis, Gladys and Vernon. Though it may have been a true event, I don't personally know this to be factual.

It has been stated by Rex Humbard that he was able to pray with Elvis prior to his death. This too may have occurred but I was not privy to the event.

The only times Elvis visited First Assembly in Memphis were those occasions when they sponsored a gospel concert. His participation in these events was motivated only by his love for gospel music. I know this to be accurate because Elvis told me so.

Elvis was a diligent searcher for eternal life truths. He constantly read books like "The Bible," "The Immortal Life," "The Impersonal Life," and others teaching various theologies. It appeared to me that he had an insatiable longing for truths as they relate to life after death.

I recall one night when Elvis motioned for me to follow him. We went into his bedroom and Elvis sat on the bed with his back to the head board and I sprawled out across the foot of the bed, on my side with my head propped up by my bent arm and said, "What 'cha need, boss?"

His response will always be the memory of a door that once opened before me and one that I failed to walk through. I was in no way a professing believer at the time and the question Elvis asked me was a total surprise. It is not within my power to return again to that point and redo it properly but I can tell you now, what was said.

Elvis asked me, "What does 'being saved' mean?"

I was astonished that Elvis would ask "me" such a question and I said back to him, "Far out boss, why ya askin' me such 'a question? Do I look like 'a preacher?"

"Seriously," he said, "I was watchin' a show on TV and they were talking about when they got 'saved.' I know your dad was a preacher and I figured if anybody here would know, you would."

Realizing, then, that he was seriously trying to determine what "being saved" really was, I made a brief attempt at trying to explain it the way that my Daddy used to preach it.

I said to Elvis, "Well, Daddy always preached that if you believe the story that Jesus really came here like everybody says He did and if you believe that He died for sins like they say He did and if you believe all the other stuff they say, like, He rose from the dead, went back to Heaven and that He's coming again some day: If you really believe all of that and 'don't' believe that there's any other way to get to Heaven, then you're saved. 'Being saved' is just a way of saying that you are a 'born again believer' and that, ya know you're gonna go to heaven."

Elvis then asked, "Well, what happens then?"

I was really getting into it by then and answered him, "Well if you do all that, by what they call 'faith,' and ya ask Jesus to take control of your livin', He will! After that He'll help you do stuff like make the right decisions and be a better kind of person." I said to him, "I've heard my daddy say, lots of times, 'If Jesus wasn't walkin' with me, I don't think I could make it'." I then concluded my "redneck" message with the comment, "But the best part is, when you die you go to heaven instead of hell!"

Elvis' short comment was, "Cool!" Then after a couple more non-essential statements were made, we returned to the living room.

I left Elvis eleven months before His death and I am now certain that the act of becoming a part of the family of God and thereby, at some point, a receiver of an eternal life in His presence only requires a split second. Elvis had numerous seconds in which to do so after my leaving if he had not already done so prior to my resignation.

"Was Elvis a Christian?" That answer lies between Elvis and God and "those two" alone.

He was my true friend and I sure hope he was.

I know that "I am" and I expectantly look forward to seeing Elvis again, "someday!"

What is being saved? Simply this truth! Truly believing and affirming that a man called "Jesus The Christ" came to earth from Heaven, lived a flawless life, died on a cross to erase all of our wrongs, was buried in a tomb and came back to life again, has gone back to Heaven and is alive now as "The Lord" and that He will return as "The King of Kings!"

As a line in an old spiritual I used to sing says: "Dat's da truth, honey babe, Dat's da truth."

"... Believe on the Lord Jesus Christ, and thou shalt be saved..." *-Acts 16:31*

"You can't rewrite history
but the future has yet to be penned!"
-Donnie

CHAPTER THIRTY TWO
A BEGINNING AT THE END

"**I** just can't take it anymore!"

I know I've said it on numerous occasions and I'm sure you have too.

In all probability, we just made the statement as an emotional release or spoke it in jest. In most cases, it was forgotten in a relatively short period of time

I recall one occasion when I truly meant it!

It was in September of 1976, at the Hilton Hotel in Vegas.

Earlier that year, on two occasions, I had tried to overdose on cocaine which resulted in Elvis sending me to a therapist who had diagnosed me as a manic depressant. I related well to the word "depressant" but I never have, to this day, really understood what he meant by "manic" unless he was referring to the maniacal manner in which I had been living my life.

For the past few months, I had been going thru about four grams of cocaine a day, eating Quaaludes like m-and-m's and smoking angel dust regularly.

On one occasion, when I had expressed my desire to "kick" drugs, Elvis said to me, "Well! If ya really want to quit, just 'suck it up, pick ya self up by the bootstraps' and quit!"

I truly wish it had been that easy but it wasn't! I

desperately wanted to stop because I'm a smart man and I had a clear view of where I was headed!

My voice was gone! I had stopped singing the high notes for Elvis and Ed Enoch, the lead vocalist in The Stamps, was singing them for me.

Tim Baty, the baritone singer in Voice, had started singing lead and I had dropped down to the baritone part.

My weight had dropped to one hundred thirty eight pounds and standing six foot four, that's rather slim.

My home had been irretrievably broken and my nights and days had become just a blur.

To this day I can't recall some of the things that my friends remind me of.

On September 10, 1976, I said what I felt and meant what I said.

"I can't take anymore!"

I was alone in my room trying to get over a wild night of drugs. I had been up all night and the sun was just coming up in Vegas.

I wanted to get some sleep but I had spent the previous few hours filling my body with so many illegal substances that sleep just wouldn't come.

I picked up the phone, called Elvis' suite and Charlie Hodge picked up the phone.

I said, "Charlie, if Elvis is still up, can I come and talk to him?" Charlie answered back, "He's already gone to his room but I'll go check." In a short bit Charlie was back on the phone and he said, "Elvis said to come on."

I got up out of bed, left my room, went to Elvis' suite and knocked on the door. Charlie answered the door, told me to come on in and then he walked over to Elvis' bedroom door, knocked on it and said, "Donnie's here."

Elvis came to the door, opened it and said, "Hey man! What's happ'nin'!"

I followed Elvis back into his bedroom, he got up on his bed in a sitting position much like an Indian beside a campfire and I assumed the same position on the floor beside his bed.

In order to have a reason for wanting to talk to him, I started asking questions about how to initiate an "out of body" experience. Knowing that this was a subject he had been reading about, I figured it would be a good way to start toward the real purpose of my visit.

Eventually, I was able to get down to what I had come to do.

I thanked Elvis for all the things he had done for me, for what he had allowed me to be and "most of all," for being a "true friend!"

Following a few more brief comments, I left Elvis' bedroom, walked thru the empty living room and out thru a set of sliding glass doors that open up to a patio on top of the Las Vegas Hilton.

Knowing what I had come to do, I walked across the patio and hoisted myself up onto a low protective wall that surrounds the roof top patio.

I was standing there looking down toward the parking lot twenty eight floors below, thinking to myself, "If I do it, "that's it! There ain't gonna be no comin' back this time!"

In truth, nobody wants to die but sometimes, the choices

that one has made will build walls around them so black and so high that death is the only avenue of escape they can see.

Even a saintly little mom, lying on her bed in a terminal condition saying, "I just wish God would take me on home!" in fact, is not wishing to die.

Whether motivated by their wish to end a problem or by their longing to enter into a state of heavenly bliss, it matters not! Dying is not what the person really wants. "Out of the present circumstance!" is what they are truly reaching for and if death seems to be the only path to that goal, they will go ahead and accept it.

Standing there that morning, twenty eight floors in the air, trying to get up enough nerve to jump, I experienced the most "hopeless moment" of my entire living.

In my heart, I didn't really want to die! I just, "desperately wanted out!"

I had been trying to "outrun" my Daddy's religion all of my life. In the process of doing so, I had experimented with every theological concept, every denomination and every religious practice that I became exposed to.

I was not an atheist but thru the years of my religious wanderings, I had truly become a "hard-hearted" agnostic. I had chosen to believe that there was a "higher power" in some form but I didn't believe it to be that which I have come to know as, "Yahweh" the all powerful "God of the Bible!"

As a last resort, I took a shot in the dark! Some might say it was sacrilegious but I was like a man going over Niagara falls, reaching for a rope!

In my drugged condition, I looked up and very loudly said, "I can't figure out who you are or what 'cha are but if there's anything to you, like my Daddy said there was, I could sure use some help!"

I can't prove it but I like to believe that My Heavenly Father was walking around on His heavenly patio that morning admiring the majesty of all the worlds that he had formed, when suddenly he heard someone, in a mess, crying out for help.

When He heard the desperate plea, He suddenly remembered a promise He had made to "all people" for "all of eternity."

The "Father of Love" remembered saying, "Call upon me in the day of trouble and I will deliver thee " -*Psalm 50:15*

He hadn't made looks, money or fame a prerequisite. He had simply said, "Who-so-ever!"

I didn't have anything pretty to offer Him but when I called out to him, there was no way He was going to break a promise He had made for He had already said of Himself, "I have spoken it ... I will do it." -*Ezekiel 36:36*

He had no other choice and on wings of mercy, He jumped from His balcony at the edge of eternity, soared down to the rooftop of the Las Vegas Hilton and with arms reaching out, He took a position right beside me!

I didn't see anything, I didn't hear anything nor was I in a "religious" frame of mind but all of a sudden, the lyrics of a song began to scroll thru my consciousness.

It was a song Mom and Dad had made me sing as a kid. I had to sing it every Sunday morning after Sunday School with all of the other kids and I had not thought of it in years. The lyrics went, "Jesus loves me this I know for the Bible tells me so" and the next line went thru my thoughts like a bullet, "Little ones to Him belong, they are weak but He is strong!"

I began to cry as hard as I've ever cried in my life and I

assumed, at the time, I was having a drug reaction. Since then, I have come to understand the reality of the moment.

My Heavenly Father, with hands of "forgiveness," was reaching down into the gutter of life and with "grace" was pickin' up a guy named, "Donnie!" With "love" he was beginning the difficult task of cleaning him up, so that someday, He could proudly introduce him to the world as, "My Child!"

It's amazing how some "little something" can so quickly cause a situation to be pointed toward another direction!

I became fearful that someone was gonna see "me" crying and I certainly didn't want that embarrassment, so, I climbed down off the little wall I was on, sneaked back thru the living room, went to my room, fell across the bed and cried myself to sleep.

When I woke up later in the day, I was still groggy from drugs but I remembered where I had been, what I had tried to do.

When I began contemplating the conclusion of that memory, I started crying again!

Praying is "not" like riding a bicycle! If you don't do it for a long period of time you just might forget the religious and ecclesiastical manner in which other folks choose to word their prayers. I certainly know that I had lost my ability to pray "like my Daddy."

Not really knowing how to be "church-like" but feeling a rather strong urge to do something that was rather foreign to me, I got off of the bed and knelt down by it in a manner similar to the way my Momma used to make me do when she prayed before we went to bed.

I had not yet learned all of the "denominational" phrases that I would later come to know, nor was I comfortable with the "theological rhetoric" that would be mine to study in the future.

I just sorta knelt there trying to figure out what I should do and finally said, "I don't really know what's goin' on 'right now but I know for sure I'd like to kick drugs and be a better person. I can't pull it off all by myself but if You'll help me to get myself straight again, I'll tell everybody that 'You' did it!"

When I got thru, my hair was still long, my eyes were still red from drugs, I still only weighed one hundred and thirty eight pounds, my home was still broken and I was still "all alone" in my room. No organ had been played, no preacher had preached and no invitational hymn had been sung but during the time it had taken to speak that rather childish prayer, something beautiful had happened!

I had been transformed into a new person! God The Father had made me a "brand new man!"

As I look back on it now, I know for certain what happened that afternoon in the quietness of my room.

"My Heavenly Father" started listening to every word I was saying that evening and without hesitation, even as I was talking to Him, He walked toward His divine wardrobe, opened it up and picked out a brand new covering of His Son's "promised" righteousness "especially for me."

As I continued to talk to Him, He gently placed the robe around my shoulders and before I was even finished, He had walked over to His eternal desk from which He had picked up His divine pen of forgiveness.

By the time I had finished, He had "already" dipped his pen into the well of His own Son's blood and had written my name "for all eternity" into His "Book of Life!"

And "that" boys and girls was the very best and the very most important event that has ever happened in my life!

My friends still remember what I used to be and what I used to do but when it comes down to the bad things they might wish to recall, My Heavenly Father has "no idea" what they're talking about! He just can't remember them anymore 'cause we got it all worked out, a long time ago, in a busy desert town called Las Vegas.

Just a few days later we all went back to Memphis.

When we got there, Elvis went into the hospital for some test concerning a procedure he was to face in a few days.

I went to see him there and just before I left, I said to him, "Boss, there's something I need to ask ya for and I really don't know how to put it."

Elvis said back to me, "Just let 'er go!"

I replied back to him, "Well Boss! You know the mess my life's been in for a while. Well, last week I decided that I'm gonna do whatever it takes to get my act straight and if you'll let me do it, with no hard feelings, I'd like to break my contract, go back to Nashville, get a normal job and try to put myself back together."

Elvis just looked at me a second and then said to me, "Far out man!" "Great move!" "I'm proud of ya!" He just sat there kinda quiet a little bit and then said, "Wow, man! I wish I could do that. I'd love to just go somewhere and start all over and be what I'd like to be but I guess I'll have to keep on bein' Elvis." Then, after a short pause, he ended by saying, "You go do what ya gotta do, my friend, and if ya ever need me, ya know how to git 'a hold of me!"

That was the last time I ever experienced the joy of speaking, face to face, with "my friend, Elvis!"

To anyone who might be finding their life to be less than desirable and to anyone who might wish they could start fresh, may I share what I have found to be some unshakable promises from One who can neither lie nor break His vow.

"He shall call upon me, and I will answer him: I will be with him in trouble; I will deliver him, and honour him." -Psalm 91:15

" ... I will forgive their iniquity, and I will remember their sin no more." -Jeremiah 31:34

**I will greatly rejoice in the LORD,
my soul shall be joyful in my God;
for he hath clothed me with the garments of salvation,
he hath covered me with the robe of righteousness" -Isaiah 61:10**

**"Therefore if any man be in Christ, he is a new creature:
old things are passed away;
behold, all things are become new." -II Corinthians 5:17**

"When you come to the end of your rope,
tie a knot in it and hang on a little longer.
God will always show up in time to catch you!"
-Donnie

CHAPTER THIRTY THREE
DADDY KEPT PRAYING

Lots of folks say prayers but there are some that "really pray!" My Daddy was part of the long and loud prayer group.

I will be the first to tell you that my Daddy's praying was not the source of my redemption but I will boldly proclaim to you that his prayers and his love kept the light of God's grace shining brightly enough on my living to show me the way back to "The Father's House" when everything else had fallen apart in my world.

I have never in my life known anyone who prayed more often or any louder than Daddy. Morning, noon and night, he prayed at least an hour each time.

Not only did Daddy pray a lot, he spent hours every day reading and studying the Bible.

What I lack in self discipline, my Daddy made up for. Among the list of dedicated and faithful members in the family of God, you will certainly find my father's name very near the top.

Daddy was both a "prayer warrior" and a "walking Bible!"

During the coarse of his life he memorized the complete New Testament and a major portion of the Old Testament. His sermons contained very few opinions. For the most part, his messages were just a continuous stream of direct quotes from the Bible. Even his conversations were interspersed with numerous Biblical quotations.

Because of my Father's zeal in the pursuit of righteousness, I tried not to be around him anymore than I had to. I was living a very reckless life and every time I saw Daddy he told me he loved me and was praying for me. I was most grateful for his love but I sure didn't want him to change my life style with praying because I was having a great time and it would be a while before I would discover the truth of *Hebrews 11:25* and realize that "the pleasures of sin" truly are but "for a season."

During his ministry my Dad fathered thirty two churches across the country and in 1976 was serving his denomination as superintendent of all the churches in their North Eastern District.

According to what my Dad has told me, he was in his office reading the Bible and "All of a sudden a scripture seemed to just jump off the page. It was *II Timothy 1:12*, 'I know whom I have believed, and am persuaded that he is able to keep that which I have committed unto him'!"

Dad said, "I began to 'weep in The Spirit' and I said to God, I know You just like Paul knew You and I am persuaded to believe that You are able just like him! I don't know what he committed to You but I'm gonna give You my son! You promised me that if I would train him up in the way he should go that You would do the rest. I've done my part and there's nothing else I can do, so, I'm gonna give him to You, 'lock, stock and barrel!' I'm gonna take you at Your promise to do the rest. I'll never 'ask you' again for His salvation but until I die, I will continually 'thank You' for it! I sure would like to see it with my own eyes and as a token of my thanksgiving, if Your will can permit it, I'm gonna eat one meal a day and 'thank You' for 'my boy's return' every time I pray until I either see his salvation or Your face!"

Daddy ate one meal a day for nine years before his prayers came to fruition and I've been told that at the start of each message during those nine years, he would ask the congregation to stand and rejoice with him over the salvation of "his son!"

The third week in September of 1976 I called my Daddy. I had not seen him since the previous Christmas. When he answered the phone I said, "Daddy this is Donnie." Dad replied, "What's wrong son, is there anything I can do to help you?" I guess he figured if it was me calling, I had to be in some sort of trouble.

I answered back with, "Everything's fine here. I just called to let you know that I'm not with Elvis anymore and I have a job driving a school bus here in Nashville." His response was, "What happened Son?"

That's when I hit him broadside with, "I got saved last week and I quit the Presley show."

I will never forget the sound of Daddy's shout followed by a quote from *Luke 2:29-30*, "Lord, let Thy servant depart in peace for my eyes have seen thy salvation!"

Thank God Daddy kept praying! "Long and loud!"

Some folks declare prayer to be an ineffective effort but I had a great teacher and have found it to be the answer to a lot of my life's problems.

"Prayer changes things" is not just a church bulletin board slogan. I do it frequently and it works!

"The effectual fervent prayer of a righteous man availeth much.". *-James 5:16*

"Whatsoever ye shall ask in my name, that will I do." *-John 14:13*

"No father stands taller than when he bends a knee to pray!"
-Donnie

CHAPTER THIRTY FOUR
STARTIN' OVER

"**F**rom The King of Rock To The King of Kings!"

That was the lead line of a newspaper article announcing my first "solo" concert, presented in Hamilton, Ohio during Thanksgiving 1977. A portion of my current press package still contains the phrase.

It looks really good on paper but the transition wasn't easy during the first few months of my "New Life."

Never-the-less, I can boldly proclaim to you that my "New Life" has certainly been the most full-filling and rewarding period of my entire living.

In an effort to get my "act" together, I left Memphis, came back to Nashville, went into drug rehab and started life all over again beneath the "shadow" of "The King of Kings!"

I had no intention of ever again pursuing full time musical performance. I thought I would like to sing in a church choir and maybe do an occasional solo in church but that was it.

I knew I had to get a job in order to eat but music was the only thing I had a broad working knowledge of and I really couldn't figure out what I should do.

My son Jeff and my daughter Robin were attending a Christian Academy in South Nashville and a couple of days after I left Elvis, I went to have lunch with them at school.

While I was visiting my kids, the principle of the school

came over and sat down with us. It was Chuck Ramsey, the pianist I had replaced when I joined The Stamps. He asked me what I was doing in town and I told him, "Right now, I'm looking for a job!" I went on to explain to him that I had resigned from the Elvis show and was about to enter a drug rehab program. Chuck jokingly said, "You used to drive the bus for The Stamps didn't ya." I answered, "Yeh!" He followed with "Ya wanna come drive a bus for Whispering Hills Christian Academy?" His statement was probably made in jest but I needed some income and to Chuck's surprise I said, "Yeh! If you're serious!"

One week I was with Elvis and the next I was running a school bus route every morning and afternoon with the remainder of my day spent in drug rehab in Madison, Tennessee. I tell folks, "I didn't have but one nerve left and twice a day thirty two kids got right in the middle of it!"

I started going to church regularly but was less than the leading parishioner. The only clothes I had were my glitzy stage clothes and a large supply of tank top shirts and blue jeans.

At the time, my shoe supply was several pairs of "Indian type" moccasins and boots.

My hair was still long and hung down past my shoulders. Looking back on myself, I suppose that I really didn't fit the profile of a "church-go'er."

The church I attended didn't welcome me with open arms. It appeared to me that they hated sin and didn't care "too much" for the sinner. My clothes and my long hair were not appropriate for participation in any of the church musical programs.

I was left pretty much alone to "root hog or die poor!"

I will always be grateful to two men who loved me, prayed for me and befriended me during those early months of my new "faith walk."

Other than my family, my first exposure to "real Christian love" came from my pastors, Rev. Wayne Proctor and Rev. Harvey Hudson, who alternately visited me everyday while I was in drug rehab and many times in my office, thereafter. The love and spiritual guidance of these two great ministers were the extended hand of God to me and on several occasions were the only reason I didn't "throw my hands up and quit!"

Right after I completed my drug rehab program, I got a G.I. haircut and with my new "Christian" haircut, I went to a discount suit store here in Nashville. I bought me two suits along with shirts, and ties as-well-as a pair of black "tie up" shoes. Now I looked "church-i-fied" and soon thereafter, folks at church began to smile at me.

There was a lot of "crawl and fall" during those early days. I didn't learn to walk on my new "church legs" immediately. It may take a while but I found out, that with determination and loving guidance, it is possible to remake one's image. By the time I left Nashville in December of 1979, to relocate in Florida, I was singing a solo during every service at my church, I was the official church pianist and the church folks were calling me, "Bro. Sumner!"

"Without the lemons there could be no lemonade!"

The beginning of my "new life" could not be described as a cake walk but I will always be grateful for a couple of great lessons I learned during my "baby Christian" months.

I had been on the road ever since my children were born and didn't know much about kids. I learned to be a "Dad" driving a bunch of little guys to and from school. When I resigned as their driver, all of my riders and their parents gave me a "going away" party. Thank God for that school bus.

In the list of "do's" that a Christian might wish to assemble, there is one that supersedes them all and that is "love!" Thank God I found it in Pastor Wayne and Pastor Harvey.

"Now abideth faith, hope, love, these three; but the greatest of these is love." -1 Corinthians 13:13

"Thou shalt love thy neighbour as thyself". -Matthew 22:39

"By this shall all men know that ye are my disciples, if ye have love one to another." -John 13:35

"If you stand up more times than you fall, you can get to anywhere you wish to go!"
-Donnie

146

CHAPTER THIRTY FIVE

I NEVER WILL BUT I DID

I once saw a picture of Jesus with an inscription beneath it that read;

> *"He was born with singing,*
> *His life was a song of love,*
> *He died in silence;*
> *If the music is to continue,*
> *'We' must be the melody"*

In December of 1979, I moved to Lakeland, Florida for the purpose of trying to restore my marriage. The final result was far different than the one that I had originally intended.

As a source of income I took a position selling advertising for a local paper and was trying to sing in a few local churches on the weekend.

About the only wonderful thing I was privileged to during those days was the joy of visiting with my children everyday and enjoying the warmth of their love.

My Nashville pastor, Rev. Wayne Proctor, had already "set me forth" into the ministry and the second month I was in Lakeland, I entered an intern program under my Lakeland pastor, Rev. Dennis McGuire. Practically all I know about the music industry, I learned from my Uncle J.D. Most of what I have practiced in the ministry, I gleaned from Pastor McGuire.

A few months after I became acquainted with Pastor McGuire, he scheduled me for my very first revival.

You remember me telling you that "God has an unusual

sense of humor!"

When I committed myself to full time ministry I never suspected that my first "real" effort would be at the location I had tried to out-run since 1947.

Yep! You guessed it! It my Daddy's first little church in Bradley, Florida!

I was scheduled from Sunday morning through the following Wednesday night. By the end of our service on Monday night, I had told the folks everything I knew at the time and for the next two nights I sang a lot and did very little talking.

During the following year and a half, I sang and spoke anyplace I could and continued working toward a reconciliation in my marriage but I had shattered too many dreams and inflicted too many hurts for it to become possible.

In December of 1981, I was appointed pastor at a small church in Bayard, West Virginia. It was in Bayard that I experienced "divine peace" for the first time in my life.

For all practical purposes I should have been miserable.

Bayard was really small and I like big towns. I love warm weather and Bayard was covered in snow more that six months of the year. I don't like being alone and I had given up on wedded bliss and had reconciled myself to remaining single.

With nothing else to do, I stayed in my office studying religious writings and theological works. God has been gracious to me in that he has granted me the ability to learn quickly and remember long. Thanks to my studies in the solitude of Bayard, West Virginia, I was able to assimilate enough Biblical knowledge to be awarded an earned Theological Doctorate degree in 1999.

Now all of my friends call me, "Dr." Former Elvis Backup Singer!

Things in life don't always go as you plan but I have discovered that when "The Father" completes a situation, it is always better than you could have done yourself.

"Trust in the Lord with all thine heart; and lean not unto thine own understanding. In all thy ways acknowledge him, and he shall direct thy paths." -Proverbs 3:5-6

"All things work together for good to them that love God, to them who are the called according to his purpose." -Romans 8:28

From time to time we all have situations arise that tend to cloud our day. Very often, in the middle of a "life storm" that ought to be traumatic for me, I have found a calm harbor in the arms of "Jesus my Peace!"

I can't calm all the storms in my life but I have found that the "Spirit of Jesus" living in me will give me the "strength" to withstand them and the "peace" to endure them.

"The peace of God, which passeth all understanding, shall keep your hearts and minds through Christ Jesus." -Philippians 4:7

"Thou wilt keep him in perfect peace, whose mind is stayed on thee." -Isaiah 26:3

"Peace I leave with you, my peace I give unto you ... Let not your heart be troubled, neither let it be afraid." -John 14:27

"Without curves in the road,
you could never drive to the top of a mountain!"
-Donnie

CHAPTER THIRTY SIX
ON THE ROAD AGAIN

It was "apple butter time in Bayard, West Virginia and I was the official "stirrer" for the ladies group in our church.

It was customary for the pastor's wife to be chair person of the ladies group at the church in Bayard. I was a single pastor and consequently, I became the "senior director" of the "ladies auxiliary."

As a fund raiser, each year the ladies made multiplied dozens of gallon jars filled with apple butter. On Monday and Tuesday, during the second week of October, 1983, the girls and I had picked several pick-up truck loads of apples and peeled them. On Wednesday we began the process of preparing the final product.

I had not yet announced it to my church but I was planning to marry a beautiful young lady from Carmi, Illinois by the name of Martha Ann McGuire. I had previously made arrangements with my state superintendent and a new pastor was to begin his tenure on the following Sunday. I made the announcement to my congregation that Wednesday night and enjoyed their kind remarks and gracious hugs before we all left for home.

I headed for Carmi early the next morning and when the girls came in to work Thursday, they found a big chalk board propped up on a table that read, "From one apple dumpling to another, I luv ya girls! Gone to get married, Donnie!"

On October 15, 1983 Marty and I said our "I do's" and we have been joined at the hip ever since. In twenty eight years we have never spent a night apart. Since 1983 she has ridden beside me every mile that I have traveled and has not missed a single service that I have conducted.

Since we joined our lives together, Marty and I have lived in several homes in several states and have traveled nearly two million miles together by car. Together we have visited practically every state in the U.S. and have slept in every major city. Sometimes the crowd was very large and sometimes it was rather small. We have enjoyed the birth of grand children and the joy of watching them become young adults. Through the years we have made thousands of friendships and experienced the rebirth of unknown numbers of folks who had lost their way in life.

Now-a-days I spend considerable time on my front porch admiring the beauty of Old Hickory Lake "waiting on Marty" to "get ready" for our next appointment.

People often ask me, "When ya gonna retire!" I tell them, "Never!"

As long as God grants me the strength and ability, I will continue to share the "good news" of the "gospel" to anyone who will listen and at any place I am given the opportunity to do so.

My effort may often sound like singing and at other times it may be rendered with a spoken word but the message will forever be the same.

In Jesus there's a "brand new life!" In Jesus there's an "abundantly blessed life!" In Jesus and in Him alone there awaits an "everlasting life!"

My name's Donnie and that's my "greatest story" and that's my "only song."

People often inquire as to my favorite scripture verse and the answer comes quickly.

"He that dwelleth in the secret place of the most High shall abide under the shadow of the Almighty" *-Psalm 91:1*

I have discovered that without a battle, there could be no victory and on numerous occasions I have relied upon the content of that verse to get me safely past a large problem that was standing in my way.

*"**Dwelleth**" is defined in the original tongue as, "to stake a claim" and further, "fight to retain possession of."*

*"**Secret Place**" is the sum total of all the "promised" provisions provided to mankind by the birth, death, resurrection and subsequent ascension of "The Messiah, Jesus The Christ."*

*"**Abide**" is interpreted as "to stay a while" and further defined as, "not the end" and "more to come."*

*"**Shadow**" is simply "A protective covering!"*

*"**The Almighty!**" "The highest of all powers: Totally self contained, all sufficient and eternally existing!"*

That's the way it reads in a theological form but may I share with you the "Donnie translation?" I have staked my hopes and aspirations in all of the "promises" made to me by my "Heavenly Father" and I expect to hang around a while and enjoy all of the "protection, provision, direction and health" that His Son, "Jesus The Christ" has made available to me.

**"I will say of the LORD, He is my refuge
and my fortress: my God;
in him will I trust.." -Psalm 91:2**

CHAPTER THIRTY SEVEN

FROM GRACELAND TO A LAND OF GRACE

Graceland has come to be known as a "national landmark" but I'll always remember it as "the home of my friend Elvis" and will often recall it as a place where "I once lived."

Having been the son of a "pastor" and having lived in numerous "parsonages" that were less than elaborate, I can tell you that Graceland, was truly something to be "greatly enjoyed!"

I recall my first time thru the front gates of Graceland.

I was in a long white limo, sitting in a jump seat facing Elvis. As we drove south on Elvis Presley Boulevard in Memphis, I remember turning left and then stopping. As we faced the gated entrance, Joe Espisito took a card from his pocket, rolled down the window and slipped the card into a little slot on the face of a small mechanism to his left.

Just like magic, the gates opened and we proceeded up the driveway toward the "mansion!"

A mansion it really was!

It had a well manicured lawn with a "smooth-as-glass" driveway circling in front of it.

Elvis' mansion had some of the biggest front doors you've ever seen.

To use a line from the movie, "Gone With The Wind," I

recall, then and many times thereafter, thinking to myself, "Lawsy, we rich now!"

I can assure you that the home of Elvis was extremely luxurious and that I "really" enjoyed my times there.

Graceland had an enormous stone wall fence along the entire frontage facing Elvis Presley Boulevard and when Elvis was in town there were always fans present.

During those times, if you stood at the front door and looked toward the wall, all you could see was a "row of eyeballs" trying to get a glimpse of Elvis.

The sad part of it was this, even though Elvis loved his fans, they couldn't come thru the gates because they weren't part of the family.

I can also recall my thoughts and feelings when I heard the gates of Graceland click behind me for the last time.

I thought to myself as I watched Graceland disappear in my rear view mirror, "Well, ole boy, you probably won't ever get to live like that again!"

Was I ever wrong!

In a short few days after that departure, I was made extremely happy when I read some lines in a book called "The Bible" that said, "Let not your heart be troubled. Ye believe in God, believe also in me. In my Father's house are many mansions. If it were not so, I wouldn't have told you. I go to prepare a place for you and if I go and prepare a place for you, I will come again, and receive you unto myself; that where I am, there ye may be also." -*John 14:1-3*

It excited me so much I began trying to find out all I could about it and in my search I discovered some amazing "facts."

I was comforted to read about a place where the driveways weren't just asphalt, they were made of "solid, transparent gold!" There were no homes there fashioned from Tennessee rocks, they were all constructed using only "solid gold" bricks. This place didn't have an entrance gate designed in wrought iron. No Sir! It had "twelve" gigantic gates, each of them hewn from an enormous pearl. These twelve beautiful gates were intermittently spaced within four gigantic walls formed only by layers and layers of crystal clear jasper.

It didn't mention any guard houses being at the gates but it said there'd be "no night there" and that all was gonna be "at peace" for ever-and-ever, so, I don't guess they need a guard house.

My reading further unfolded to me the fact that when you come inside the place, no one will ever need a "hankie" 'cause all tears will cease to exist.

After reading long and hard trying to find mention of a local mortuary facility, I became joyful when I came across a notice that assured me there would be no "dying" inside this exquisite "gated" community.

At one point, I was saddened by the fact that "not everyone" would be allowed to become a resident: Titles were only being granted to "family members!"

What a joy it was to discover that "adoption into the family" was an extremely easy formality.

I was further elated when I noticed the good news that there were plenty of grants still available and that they were "free of charge" to anyone who might wish to apply.

I checked out the application and very little was required.

The document was both short and simply composed.

Here, boys and girls, is the total form:

**"Believe on the Lord Jesus Christ,
and thou shalt be saved"** *-Acts 16:31*

**"If thou shalt confess with thy mouth the Lord Jesus,
and shalt believe in thine heart
that God hath raised him from the dead,
thou shalt be saved."***-Romans 10:9*

**"God so loved the world, that he gave his only
begotten Son, that whosoever believeth in him
should not perish,
but have everlasting life."** *-John 3:16*

That's all I did and I found out "it works!"

I just said within my own consciousness;

*"God, I've made some pretty big mistakes in my life
but I believe your Son, Jesus, died to take care of all that.
I sure would like to start over
and try to make something good out of all my messes.
I'm asking Your Son, Jesus,
to take charge of my thinking and my actions.
I'm gonna try to do things right from now on
and if You'll help me do it;*

I'LL TELL EVERYBODY THAT 'YOU' DID IT!"

He did and I'm gonna!

"Thanks" boys and girls for continuing with me thru my entire exhibit and I trust that you have enjoyed viewing all of the portraits that I prepared for ya'. Just before you exit the museum may I share with you the "main" purpose for which I extended to you an invitation to be a part of my world.

As my friend, I simply wanted you to be assured of this: **"For all that I am and all that I will ever become: For everything I have and everything I shall ever receive; I must proclaim, "TO GOD BE THE GLORY" for it all." I AM ONLY BECAUSE "JESUS IS!"**

I'm still "just a singer" but really, I'm "somebody special" because I am "now" an "adopted" member in my Heavenly Father's family.

I'm still "not rich" but my Heavenly Father "owns it all" and has promised to "supply all my needs" according to all that He has.

I'm still not handsome but someday I have the "promise" of a "new and perfect body" for all of eternity.

Yes friend, it truly has been a "wonderful life" and I look forward to the day when my "greatest dream" comes true. It's a very simple dream and I am confident it will come to pass.

Here it is!

When time makes the final change in me, I dream of entering into my Heavenly Father's "Land of Grace" and enjoying eternity with my "entire family," along with "Elvis" and "all of you."

It's gonna be great! For at least ten million years we'll all sit down in a golden living room, on golden chairs around a golden piano and sing like there'll be no tomorrow because "there won't be."

I'll see ya there!

This story has no end!

*"... and they shall reign
for ever-and-ever."*

-Revelation 22:5

*"Of the increase of his government
and peace
there shall be no end."*

-Isaiah 9:7

DONNIE
2012

PHOTO
GALLERY

FRANK SUMNER
1940
The Father I Never Knew

PETE
FRANCES
DONNIE
1994

DONNIE
FRANCES
J.D.
PETE
1996

MOM AND DAD 1943
Just Before They Adopted Me

DADDY 1944
He Was Proud of His Fruit Truck

MOM AND DAD
1947
Shortly Before
Dad Enrolled In College

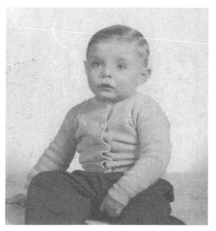

MY BIRTHDAY
1945

MY BIRTHDAY
1946

ME IN DADDY'S BOAT
SUMMER OF 51
Just Before Moving
To Bradley, Florida

I Never Have Gotten Over
My Love For Fishing

OUR MOBILE ESTATE
Waiting To Be Pulled To Cleveland, Tennessee
JULY, 1947

MY BIRTHDAY
1947

I ALWAYS HAVE BEEN
A STYLISH DRESSER

A Preacher's Kid
1948

DAD AND I
On Lookout Mountain
Chattanooga, Tennessee
EARLY 1948

THE HOUSE I RAN AWAY FROM
AT DADDY'S FIRST REVIVAL
1948

SHARON AND I
The Easter King and Queen
BRADLEY, FLORIDA
1952

SCHOOL PIC
1953

Why Do They Call Me
One Ear Duck

SCHOOL PIC
1954

I'm Not Mean
I'm Just Mischievous

SCHOOL PIC
1955

Say What!

*OUR FAMILY
MIAMI,
FLORIDA
1953*

*THE PASTOR'S
FAMILY
CRISFIELD,
MARYLAND
1957*

*MY LAST FAMILY PIC
Just Before
Headin' for College
EASTON,
MARYLAND
1960*

DADDY - 1959

DADDY - 1993

MY LAST PICTURE
WITH MOM AND DAD TOGETHER
2007

MY LAST PICTURE
WITH DADDY
2007

THE SONGSMEN
1960

THE SONGSMEN
1963

THE STAMPS TRIO
1964

THE STAMPS QT.
1965

THE STAMPS QT.
1966

THE STAMPS QT.
1966

THE STAMPS QT.
1967

THE STAMPS ON STAGE 1971
Just Before We Joined Elvis

J.D. AND ELVIS
BACKSTAGE LAS VEGAS
1975

J.D. SUMNER
1978

DONNIE
AND
JEFF
1996

"My
Son"

"MY PRIDE AND JOY"

"My
Daughter"

DONNIE
AND
ROBIN
1996

JEFF, ROBIN AND DONNIE - 1993
Singing Together at the Gatlinburg Convention Ctr.

DONNIE
AND
JEFF
On Stage
ELVIS WEEK
MEMPHIS
1994

JEFF
AND
DONNIE
Practicing On Stage
ELVIS WEEK
MEMPHIS
1995

THE STAMPS QUARTET
RICK STRICKLAND, JEFF SUMNER
ED HILL and J.D. SUMNER
On Stage
AT DOLLYWOOD
GATLINBURG, TENNESSEE
1997

THE STAMPS
With Our New
T.C.B.'s
1971

THE STAMPS
WITH ELVIS
Backstage

LAS VEGAS
1972

THE STAMPS
In Front Of The Marquee
LAS VEGAS HILTON
1971

THE RANGERS - 1973

VOICE -1975

Sean Nielsen – Tim Baty – Donnie Sumner

ELVIS AND VOICE
On Stage At The Astrodome
HOUSTON, TEXAS - 1974

ON TOUR 1974

**ON TOUR
1975**

LAS VEGAS 1976

DONNIE
July
1976

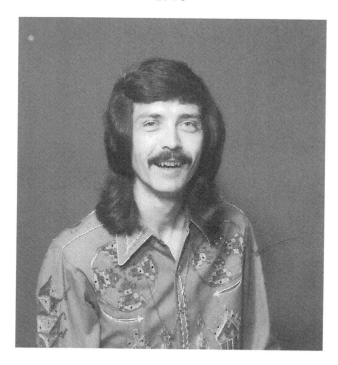

ELVIS WEEK AUGUST - 2002
Cast Reunion
MEMPHIS, TENNESSEE

DONNIE and MARTY
1984

DONNIE and MARTY
1988

DONNIE and MARTY
1989

MY GRADUATION
From
Southern Bible Institute and Seminary
AUGUSTA, GEORGIA
1999

DR. DONNIE H. SUMNER Th. D.

"For all that I am
and all that I shall become"

"For all that I have
and all that I shall receive"

I say:

"TO GOD BE THE GLORY
FOR IT ALL!"

Published By

LIFE LINE BOOKS
Hendersonville, TN 37077

ALL RIGHTS RESERVED
© 2012 by Spirit Ministries

18312968R00099

Made in the USA
Charleston, SC
27 March 2013